Challenges to the Dream

The Best of the
Martin Luther King, Jr. Day Writing Awards
at Carnegie Mellon University

_____

Edited by Jim Daniels

Carnegie Mellon University Press
Pittsburgh 2017

Acknowledgments

These awards would have never gotten off the ground or managed to survive for all these years without the generous support of Carnegie Mellon University, and many, many individuals at the university—students, staff, administrators, and faculty—who have been instrumental in keeping this program going.

First, thanks to M. Shernell Smith, Assistant Director of Student Affairs. Shernell came on board at a crucial point and helped take the writing awards to the next level when they were in danger of disappearing entirely.

Special thanks to the Dietrich College of Humanities and Social Sciences for its generous financial support of the awards, and of this anthology.

I want to thank present and former English Department colleagues Kevin González, Yona Harvey, Terrance Hayes, Jane McCafferty, and Richard Purcell, who all spent time directing or working on the awards over the years; English Department heads David Kaufer, Christine Neuwirth, and Andreca Ritivoi; Deans John Lehoczky and Richard Scheines; Presidents Jared Cohon and Subra Suresh; University staff members Stefanie Johndrow, Amanda King, and Shilo Rea; Anne Witchner, Assistant Dean of Student Affairs, who helped get the awards started back in 1999; English Department research assistants Kitty Shropshire, Larissa Briley, Katherine Frazier, Kyle Sofianek, Kate Mashek, and Emily Rodgers; Carnegie Mellon Sigma Tau Delta members who helped with judging; Gerald Costanzo, Cynthia Lamb, and Connie Amoroso at Carnegie Mellon University Press, for their support of and belief in this anthology; and all the students and their teachers who have made these awards possible.

Library of Congress Control Number 2017942692
ISBN 978-0-88748-628-9
Book design by Noah Adler and Shaune Marx
Printed and bound in the United States of America

Participating Schools

Taylor Allderdice High School
Brashear High School
Carrick High School
Central Catholic High School
Fox Chapel High School
The Kiski School
Langley High School
Lincoln Park Performing Arts Charter School
The Neighborhood Academy
Barack Obama Academy of International Studies
Oakland Catholic High School
Our Lady of the Sacred Heart High School
Peabody High School
Penn Hills High School
Perry Traditional Academy
Pittsburgh High School for the Creative and Performing Arts
Pittsburgh Science and Technology Academy
Schenley High School
Seton-LaSalle High School
Sewickley Academy
Shadyside Academy
Winchester Thurston School
Sewickley High School
Westinghouse High School
Woodland Hills High School
Carlow University
Carnegie Mellon University (Pittsburgh and Silicon Valley)
Chatham University
The Community College of Allegheny County
Duquesne University
The University of Pittsburgh

Contents

Introduction

This anthology celebrates the Martin Luther King, Jr. Day Writing Awards at Carnegie Mellon University, a poetry and prose writing contest that since 1999 has invited Pittsburgh-area high school and college students to write honestly and creatively about race. I am delighted to present a selection of their powerful work here, and to reflect on our ongoing endeavor to encourage it. When we designate a day, a week, or a month to deal with one issue, the point is often made that we should be just as thoughtful throughout the year. We take this challenge very seriously in relation to our writing awards and hope the publication of this anthology will help extend these conversations.

Some history: in graduate school at Bowling Green State University, I took a course from James Baldwin in which he challenged us to examine honestly our own backgrounds and experiences with race. At the time, less than a year removed from working at an auto plant in the Detroit area that was rife with racial tensions, I was not up to Baldwin's challenge. Later, in what I have always imagined as late work for that class, I struggled to write about my own experiences growing up as a white kid in Warren, Michigan, in the 1960s—a place for white flight after the Detroit riots in 1967.

In 1994, I edited the anthology *Letters to America: Contemporary American Poetry on Race* in an attempt to bring writers of all backgrounds together to examine the issues that often divide us. In 1999, I approached Carnegie Mellon with the idea of this community-based writing contest as a continuation of that work, a project the university generously embraced.

The mission of the MLK Day Writing Awards is to create a space for daring, eloquent, and inventive work, in the belief that the process of writing itself can help young people explore and break down issues of difference in their lives. In the spirit of Baldwin's own literary project, the contest invites high school and college students to write *personal narratives on race*, not Wikipedia-based pieces confirming Martin Luther King, Jr. as a great man or condemning racism—most of us share those beliefs already. But if we learn each other's stories, the less-visible barriers begin to break down, allowing us to see each other as thoughtful human beings, struggling, the way we all must, to live good lives and treat each other decently.

These awards are the central, signature event on our campus that day. The contest winners read in the Cohon University Center's main ballroom to an audience of hundreds who come together to listen to a diverse range of voices and perspectives. Like any attempt to discuss race in this country, the writing awards have always been less than perfect. While we receive hundreds of entries each year, they come from a fraction of the high school students in Western Pennsylvania. We constantly strive to involve more students, teachers, and schools, to help them fit this important writing into already packed curricula. In spite of these challenges, fresh young voices have, each year, risen to be heard.

Because of the sensitive nature of our subject, the submissions have on occasion stirred controversy. Some of the pieces include offensive language; many of these students have had offensive, unacceptable slurs directed at them in their daily lives. We value and honor the students' attempts to tell honest, individual stories—sometimes separating themselves from views held within their own families and communities. Their attempts, however imperfect, take brave steps to avoid the poisonous silence that Dr. King warned against.

Making these selections was extremely difficult—as it is every year for the contest judges. I hope the work included here represents both the range and the quality of what we have received over eighteen years. We reward students who struggle with complexities rather than rely on oversimplification and platitudes. In selecting these pieces, I have kept this value in mind, and I give my renewed and sincere appreciation to all of the students who have entered.

In the 1994 introduction to *Letters to America*, I listed a few of what were then recent racial incidents to show how far we are from solving our racial problems. Sadly, it would be easy—too easy—to replace those examples with many more from recent history. Perhaps it is naïve to hope that this collection might be used by teachers and students in other locations to keep the conversation going. To quote a long poem I wrote on race (long, for I had repressed much): "I am trying to be naïve . . . / Naïve enough to keep from being rolled / into another bitter pill."

I do know that in a crowded, buzzing ballroom on Carnegie Mellon's campus on Martin Luther King, Jr. Day each year, people come together and listen. I doubt that this diverse audience of readers and listeners—Pittsburgh-area families, students, and teachers; Carnegie Mellon students, staff, and faculty (who hail from all over the world)—would ever find another occasion to share the same space during their lifetimes. We are collectively, annually, moved by what we hear.

So, I invite you into their words, into the struggles of young people trying to make sense of a world in which they encounter difference, discrimination, pride, and prejudice. I have no slogan or easy message to offer. Slogans and easy messages do not win Martin Luther King, Jr. Day Writing Awards. All I can ask you to do is what all of us need to do: listen.

For more information, please visit our website: http://www.cmu.edu/dietrich/english/mlk.

Jim Daniels
Thomas Stockham Baker University Professor of English
Carnegie Mellon University

The Ink That Gives the White Page a Meaning

Amma Ababio
First Place for High School Prose, 2015

I was born in the heart of the Ashanti region in Ghana during the second term of Jerry Rawling's reign. I was sheltered from the violence and corruption that occurred around me. I was a privileged child; I did not live in a shack made of mud and sticks. I did not have to beg on the street in order to provide money for my family. I did not have to walk miles to collect water from a stream in a clay pot to drink. I did not have to cry myself to sleep because I was hungry. I lived in a lavish apartment with my parents and two sisters. My parents both had successful businesses. There was running water to drink when I was thirsty. I had housekeepers who would make me food when I was hungry. I was surrounded by loving people who looked and sounded like me.

When I was four, my father won visas in the lottery. I remember my mother telling me that I could not shave my hair anymore because little girls in America did not have bald heads. That meant that I could not take the monthly trip with my father to the barbershop to get my hair cut. Instead, I went to the hair salon with my mother to get my hair braided. In what seemed like just days, I went from playing soccer with my cousins to the Ghanaian embassy. I held tightly to my mother's hand until we were in the German airport. In an instant, I lost her hand. I walked aimlessly around the airport for half an hour. I was overwhelmed by the sea of white faces I saw. I began to think that I would never see my family again. One of the police officers that saw me projected my face on the various screens around the airport. I saw those same white faces finally stop to look at me. They looked at me with pity and asked me a series of questions. I cried even harder because I did not know what they were saying. A wave of relief came over me when I saw my father's face among a crowd of police officers. He held me close, and I did not let go of my mother's hand again.

For seven months we lived in my eldest uncle's basement until my parents found employment. In the first day alone I realized that I was no longer in Ghana. I was accustomed to eating my meals with my hands, but my aunt called me a bush girl every time she saw me eat with my hands. My favorite dish was fufu: it gave me comfort and reminded me of home.

However, my cousin called me various names until I convinced myself that fufu was disgusting. I began to eat rice like her to stop her from taunting me. One evening my uncle made Jell-O for my sister and me to try. I did not want to try it, but my uncle insisted. He took a spoonful and tried to feed it to me; I refused. He grabbed my arm and forced the red Jell-O into my mouth. I felt the spoon clink on my teeth as the Jell-O stuck to my throat. I gasped for air and wriggled free from his grip. I ran away from him as quickly as I could; I did not want him to see me cry. When my parents were able to make enough money to rent our own apartment, I was relieved that I did not have to be in that house for another day.

We moved into our new apartment in the spring of 2003. It was cramped and reeked of a concoction of different illegal drugs, but it was ours. I was comforted by the three families nearby that were also recent Ghanaian immigrants. I was able to help my parents decorate the apartment to resemble the one we had back home. Since I moved from Penn Hills to East Liberty, I had to change schools. Fulton Traditional Academy was a short walk away. I held on to my father and eldest sister's hands as we walked into school every morning. First grade was not as difficult as kindergarten because I knew how to speak English well. The English language no longer segregated me from my peers.

My parents did not speak English around my sister and me. When they picked us up from school they spoke our native Twi. I responded to them in English; I did not want my friends to know that I was not born in the United States. I had a slight accent, but no one picked up on it. My name was the only clue to my Ghanaian roots. My kindergarten teacher Americanized my name by calling me Uh-Mah, and only Uh-Mah. She did not even attempt my last name. At the tender age of six, I was no longer Amma Beniwaa Nyarko Ababio, but Uh-Mah. I was repulsed by the sight and sound of my name.

As I went through middle school and my freshman year of high school, my name was not the only aspect of my identity that repulsed me. I was disgusted by the coarseness of my hair, the hand-me-down clothes I wore, and especially the color of my skin. I caked my face with harsh skin-lightening formula and prayed that my skin would be as light as my friends'. I wore heavy, black jackets in the summer to avoid the sun's rays on my skin. However, the lightening formula worked slowly, so I resorted to baby powder; I mixed it with water and smeared it on my face. I could only apply the powder in the darkness because I was scared that the light would darken my skin. Over time I changed myself to the point that I could not bear to look at myself in the mirror. I was afraid of the person that would look back at me. I only wanted to look like the American teenage girl: white-skinned with blond hair and blue eyes.

During a discussion in my sophomore English class, one of my peers denounced the Igbo culture in the novel *Things Fall Apart*, by Chinua Achebe, as barbaric and uncivilized. My world history textbook devoted a measly two pages to ancient African history. I scoffed at their ignorance and cultural incompetence. Over a plate of jolf rice I told my eldest sister about my textbook, and my peer's comments.

She laughed, "I don't know why you care. Ain't like you know anything about Ghana either."

I rattled off the main imports and exports of the country. Then she asked me, "What you know that ain't from Wikipedia?"

I was silent.

She was right; I knew nothing about the country that I left behind in elementary school. I knew nothing of the Ashanti region I was born in, or the rich culture of the Ashanti people. I knew nothing about who I was, but I knew everything about who I could not become.

I took it upon myself to do what my textbook could not: write a thorough history of the Ashanti people. It began as a project to fulfill a requirement for my world history class, but it ultimately became my redemption. I conducted research online, then in the library, but I was dissatisfied by the information they gave me. My father was delighted when he read the description of my project. Over dinner one night he told me about my paternal grandmother, after whom I was named, Amma Nyarko. My grandmother was one of the main advisors to the king of my father's village, *Akrofuom*. Before her, four of my grandmothers founded four cities: *Huntaitai, Sikaman, Amankyim,* and *Akrofuom*. My grandmothers who founded the first city were slaves who were able to escape from their shackles. I could not find any written documentation of my grandmothers in either the library or on the Internet. When I wrote down their stories, I felt the essence of my grandmothers inside of me.

I presented my research to my peers in my world history class. I attempted to educate them about my culture, but they did not understand the significance of it. Eight days after my presentation, my peers asked me if I lived in a shack made of mud and sticks, if I had to beg on the street in order to provide money for my family, if I had running water to drink, and if I had to go to bed hungry. Their questions filled me with rage, but then I realized that it was not their fault that they had those misconceptions. My presentation was not enough to erase the countless misconceptions they had about my country and my continent as a whole. Their fatal misconceptions were shaped by America's cultural incompetency. I could present to them a hundred times, but my attempts would be futile, because my presentation was overshadowed by their misconceptions. I finally saw that my culture was a speck of dust in their eyes that they will continuously wipe away.

As a poor, young, black woman in the polarized White-Supremacist-Capitalist-Patriarchy—as Gloria Watkins names it—I have only two options. I can either be a subordinate to my white counterparts, or assimilate into a society that is lethal to my developing mind. In the words of Jean Genet, in his memoir *Prisoner of Love,* "In white America, the Blacks . . . are the ink that gives the white page a meaning."

My grandmothers were not the ink that gave the white page a meaning in Ghana. Like my grandmothers, I refuse to be the ink that gives the white page a meaning. I refuse to lose my dignity, self-respect, and identity to assimilate into a society that does not respect who I am and the culture that I embody.

Harriet Faid

Connie Amoroso
Honorable Mention for College Poetry, 2004

I.
Dear Harriet,
I have dreamt about you recently.
I see you standing on the front porch
of your grandmother's house on Friendship Avenue.
There is wind in your red curls
that sweeps locks of it into your mouth.
And you are leaning over the railing,
looking for Salvatore to stride past
on his way home from working at the theater.
It makes you giggle that he is so proud of his
ushering job, that he wears the cherry red jacket
all the time. So much so that the girls up
and down the street and at church call him
Sal Rex and smile at him as they affectionately
pat his broad shoulders underneath the uniform.
But you know that he is sweet on you, Harriet.
All the Italian mothers call out to him, fetching Sal Rex
to court their daughters, but he only stops on your
porch to ask you to the show. He only saves the best
seats in the house for you and his sister, Maria,
even though Maria will not speak to you
in her broken English. She has been taught not to speak to
Micks, not even at Mass, let alone the movie theater.
I watch you when he finally asks you to marry him, Harriet;
he wants to take you away from the neighborhood
where everyone thinks that the whispers go unheard.
He says you are Catholic, and it does not matter which kind.
Oh, and you say yes! Yes, yes, please, let's go anywhere.
Let's go there together!

II.
Dear Harriet,
I know what happened
to your children.
I know that the Great Depression made it impossible
to leave Morningside.
I know what Sal Rex's mother said about you,
and all the other Italian mothers and daughters,
so jealous even after so many years.

They said you drank whiskey straight from the bottle
hidden under the kitchen table.
Said you beat the children in fits of rage.
Said you took up with the Irish pub owner
on Liberty Avenue, only a block down
from the Rex Theater.
I see your swollen red eyes, the anger.
After four years, he started hearing them too,
and Sal Rex took both children, Salvatore and Katherine,
and moved in with his sister Maria and her husband Donato.
You had no power there; they would not even curse
at you in English when you drove over in the middle
of the night, coming to claim your son and daughter.
Your grandmother died, Harriet, and you took everything
she owned and moved to a boarding house.
You had no voice, no friends, no children anymore.
I know that when Sal Rex died a few years later in the flu epidemic,
no one told you. And Salvatore and Katherine were juggled around
friends and family in the old neighborhood. They did not even know
who was blood, everyone was Aunt or Uncle regardless.
There was no Mother.
No one told you when Katherine died at twenty-one
of tuberculosis. You read it in the newspaper,
but could not even find her grave. They wouldn't
answer your letters.

III.
Dear Great-Grandmother,
I have found you after so many years.
But all I have is Social Security records and the old stories,
finally corrected.
You lived until 1948; you never remarried, never had any other children.
My father told me that as far as he knew, you had been dead
his entire life; his family was brought up to believe that
you ran out on Sal Rex.
Do you know that you have four grandchildren?
Do you know that you have seven great-grandchildren?
Do you know that while I am proud of my Italian heritage,
that my mother is half Irish herself?
Do you know that I am proud of you?

Soljah

Katheryn (Casey) Artz
Honorable Mention for High School Prose, 2003

I never liked to dance. I tried ballet and jazz when I was about six, but these were too graceful and frilly for me. I was more of a tomboy, growing up with two older brothers. My idea of dance changed, though, one winter evening at a Peabody High School basketball game. I was only in eighth grade, but I was attending with my brother, Andy, who was a senior. The Highlanders were winning, and it was halftime. Instead of cheerleaders taking the floor, a group of eight black girls appeared, wearing Timberland boots, red camouflage pants with baggy side pockets, camo hats hanging at the back of their necks, and T-shirts reading "Peabody Steppin' Soljahs." Their boots stomped on the gym floor in unison, their hands clapped and whirled in complicated formations, the spectators gyrated to the beats that apparently were from well-known songs because the whole crowd was singing along. Some were stomping their feet on the bleachers along with the eight soldiers. By the end of the performance, sweat was beading on their faces and all chests were heaving. Never once had they taken a break. As they "stepped" out of the gym, the hollering crown applauded wildly. From that moment, I had rhythms stuck in my head and a desire to be a "Soljah."

Although I wasn't brave enough to join the step team the next fall as a freshman, I gathered my courage in tenth grade, and when step practices started in November, I went. One of my friends had promised to try out with me, but she was a dedicated swimmer and the two practice times overlapped. I was left to try out without a friend. There were six other girls at the tryouts, all black. I felt really out of place. They gave me looks, and one even asked, "Are you trying out for this?"

We began with "simple" drills, but they weren't simple for me. I had a lot of trouble combining the hand and foot routines. I had to be taught over and over, and it was frustrating. None of the girls talked to me. Other students, watching us practice in the cafeteria, whispered, "What's that white girl doin'? She think she can step?"

I worked on the drills at home, determined to master this challenge, be accepted, and perhaps even make a friend on the team. It was actually in the shower that it all came together for me. Some people do their best thinking in the shower; I only get clean. That night, though, soaking wet, trying not to slip, I suddenly got the rhythm of the two beats and my hands and feet were in sync.

By the Saturday of our first competition, I knew our routine perfectly. While we waited to go on stage, some of the girls talked to me for the first time.

"Your hair looks nice," Gigi said. Andi told me I "wasn't a bad stepper."

Even Tasha finally said something to me. "K-C, you know I didn't like you when you first came." I had no response. "I thought you were trying to be someone you ain't and it was funny when you couldn't get the drills." I still didn't know what to say. "You're not bad now, though, and I guess I got some respect for you. You're pretty decent."

I was stunned. She had never said anything directly to me, and now the "leader" of the team was accepting me. I felt really good and smiled to myself for not giving up.

As we took the stage, my heart was thumping, and I felt sick to my stomach. Our pounding feet echoed through the auditorium. At one point our steps got all mixed up, but we got our routine back together and had a strong finish. We won the competition!

From then on, I was accepted as part of the group. At practice, we all talked and laughed, and if any of them were going to a party or dance, they invited me. As a community service project, we all did the AIDS Walk together and had fun stepping and power-walking through the streets. In school, Gigi, Rhonda, and Statia even started saying "hi" to me in the halls. They all seemed proud to have me on the team. I was proud, too.

Apologies

Rachel Belloma
Honorable Mention for High School Prose, 2004

When I was younger, when my brother was even younger still, he would throw these horrible tantrums and scream and pound his fists on his head and body and the walls. In an ice cream store, he flailed wildly on the floor. This was when we were really learning about what he had. A doctor suggested my mother have cards printed up to hand out to strangers who witness his tantrums. Please excuse my son for he suffers from autism, characterized by self-absorption, inability to interact socially, repetitive behavior, and language dysfunction. My mother couldn't bear to do this. She thought it was disgusting—asking people to forgive her son for something that she didn't need to be sorry for.

My brother didn't speak for years. When he did, it was scrambled up like mixed wires in a telephone call: words were smashed together and broken into bits. My brother was barely a year younger than me, and yet he was an infant to me, still struggling with speech. I felt like his protector. On the bus once, some kids were taking his hat and bag. I grabbed him and screamed at them and swore and sounded tougher than I ever had before.

I fought and was punched in the eyebrow by an ugly kid named Brian, and I bled and it swelled up. I called him horrible names, called him a piece of trash from Lawrenceville. I made him want to fight me instead of my brother. This was when I learned how to transfer that, how to protect him by taking it onto myself. While I ended up with the swollen eye, they left him alone and fought with me. He couldn't fight back, but I could.

We didn't know what to expect from him. Maybe he'd never really talk and maybe he'd never stop throwing tantrums. He saw speech doctors and went to a different school and the tantrums slowed down, became less intense each time. There were still times when he'd shout and hit himself, always somewhere public—a department store. I overheard a clerk, rubbing her forehead, saying she didn't think she should have to deal with "that retard." It still stung, because someone was always asking to be apologized to. Card or not—when my mother looked around the store, pushing her palm into my brother's hot forehead and trying to calm him—there was an apology. I'm sorry he is like this, I'm sorry.

Ghost Dance

Rachel Belloma
Second Place for High School Prose, 2005

The night my mother met my father she asked where he came from. He said, "McKees Rocks." She said, "No, I meant what country." My father was not surprised. While living in Pittsburgh, he has been Mexican, Korean, Cuban. Nobody recognized his Cherokee face, not even my mother.

My mother's family is legend in our house. I was young when she told me how much I looked like my grandmother, brushing my hair in front of the mirror. My grandmother, she told me, was the granddaughter of Benjamin Harrison, who was a President once. In eighth grade, my teacher, who was young and believed in exposing the history of our country, read from *Bury My Heart at Wounded Knee*. In the massacre of 150 Sioux, Benjamin Harrison had sent the order down. Sioux women, Sioux children. It was all I could think of. It was a disgust I could not ignore. I look too much like my grandmother.

When I sought refuge in my father's history, he had none to offer. All my father had was a childhood with a dying father, a run-off mother, and nights he spent in a dark apartment feeling more alone than I can even imagine. He never knew his Cherokee name. There were no headdresses, no ghost dances, no funny names in my father's life. A face with no history, a Cherokee—too common—who knew nothing and felt he had nothing to know.

My father is gone now. I cannot find a textbook to fill in the blanks of his family tree, of their place in American history. I do not even look enough like him that I can prove to myself that this secret part of me exists: this unexplainable history, this tribal blood. When I see my own face, I see my mother and my mother's family and Georgia and Louisiana and never, ever Virginia or reservations in the West. I am forever sitting in front of the mirror, my mother brushing my blond hair, thinking how much I look like the Harrisons. In the mirror, I am nothing more than a silly white girl. Only in a set of lidless eyes (that are sometimes confused for Asian) am I at all a part of my father, only in that am I at all Cherokee.

When I sit at a table with a Jewish boy and his mother (who worries that someday her grandchildren will look in the mirror and not see their history), all I can think of is my father. This boy's mother, who lost parts of her family tree in Europe, looks at me and sees birthrates and baptisms and not my Cherokee father at all. When she tells her son that he shouldn't see me, I want to tell her that I know something about disappearing people.

Stranger

Maya Best
Honorable Mention for High School Poetry, 2013

Her skin,
An olive brown.
With long wispy strands of black hair
Clinging to the back of her knitted sweater.
Her brown eyes
Fixed to the ground,
Avoid eye contact.
They're all looking,
Whispering,
Wondering.
Who is the new girl?
With the mysterious eyes
And dark long hair.
She looks foreign.
Where could she come from?
I'm Indian.
Her voice heavily accented.
Eyebrows shoot up.
Could she be
Like the people from history class?
The ones who lived in America?
She squirms in her seat,
Sweaty palms clinging together.
Her head shakes no,
That's Native American.
Her whisper,
Barely audible in the classroom.
Another girl, superior,
Claims she understands.
The new girl finally relaxes.
Indians have red things on their foreheads, right?
Her face, now red,
I don't know what you mean. . . .
But she does.
The "bindis" worn on special occasions,
A type of jewelry,
Not a feature,
Like black hair,
Or a brown birthmark under a chin.

They'd never understand,
Her family going to the temple,
Bright festivals,
Shrines with flower offerings,
Singing and dancing,
If only they knew
The Bengali she spoke.
They'd ask her to say a few words,
And then mimic them.
She doesn't answer,
Letting her cheeks redden,
Two hot chili peppers.
Dreaming of disappearing,
From the whispers and stares,
Into the cool air,
With the trees that never seem to care
Where she came from,
Or the color of her hands.

One Person Wonder

Ashley Birt
First Place for College Prose, 2006 (Tie)

"Tell me, how do you feel about slavery?"

For a good majority of people, the answer to this is some variant of, "It's bad." Some may elaborate on the historical ramifications. Others may respond with a simple, "Well, no one likes it, right?" All of the above would be appropriate responses.

"I'm not saying anything," is mine.

Freshman year of college was the first time anyone asked me that. I sat in the back of my Carnegie Mellon classroom, my eyes weary from waking up so early, my head tucked beneath my arms to make sure that I was never at the teacher's eye level. If she never saw me, she could never call on me, participation grade be damned. On one particularly chilly day, I huddled in my spot, wrapped up in extra coats, completely hidden from anyone's view. Make that almost completely hidden. Apparently, my teacher didn't want my participation grade to be a zero, so she attempted to bring me into the article discussion. On slavery.

As I raised my head, I focused my eyes on the people around me. My heart began to race and I sank underneath my desk. No one, except for me, was black.

High school had never put me in this situation. About 60 percent of the students there were black. Others varied from white American to Chinese to Bulgarian to Indonesian. Everywhere you went—the hallways, the bathrooms, the bus stops—had black people. Even my higher-level courses, which were known for lacking diversity, had at least one or two other black students. When I graduated, I decided to stay not only in the same city but also in the same neighborhood. Yet within a year, I discovered that the diversity from that one building did not extend all the way down to Carnegie Mellon's campus. College, for me, is only a short walk from my high school, but that short walk is the difference between reality and a parallel universe.

I'm not saying I'd like to be in a class of only black students. Even if I had that option, I would turn it down. I like people who are different from me; if everyone I know is the same, I will never grow as a person, and then life will prove pointless. What I don't like is being the only different person drowning in the sea of sameness. What makes it worse is that, for some of my classmates, I'm the first black person they've ever seen. Suddenly, I'm their tour guide, their expert—their gateway to a strange, new culture. I cease to be a person, but rather an icon: the ultimate representative of all things black. Me, who takes pride in listening to "whiney white boys with guitars," who prefers chicken vindaloo to fried chicken; I'm supposed to represent the culture that the media paints as a bunch of baggy-pants-wearing, slang-speaking, ghetto-fabulous "pimps and hoes." Now, this image is the furthest thing from the truth, but if that's the type of person they expect me to be, they've got a surprise in store. I cannot and will not be what they want me to be. By now, I've stopped being annoyed by this and started feeling pity; anyone who wants me to represent my race is certainly misguided.

Once in a class, we discussed the use of the n-word in *The Adventures of Huckleberry*

Finn. My professor, a white man, had no idea whether he could read the word, afraid of offending any black students in his class. I went to raise my hand to say that, since it's part of the book, it didn't matter. I then remembered back to high school and thought about how this man would have fit in there. He was stiff and stodgy, fitting the stereotype associated with aging white men. His understanding of race relations appeared to be zip; while he could go on and on about the facts dealing with slavery and such things, not once had he ever spoken of it from an empathetic perspective. Rather than, "It was bad, let's figure out why," he approached it as "it was." The fact that he was even asking this question suggested that he didn't quite get the distinction between a group and a person. He didn't appear to be the most aware or approachable man, and I could imagine a situation where some of the blacks in my classes would have either complained about him to the school's authorities or left him hanging from a locker. Slowly, though without any hesitation, I lowered my hand.

My silence doesn't come from a lack of opinion. *The Adventures of Huckleberry Finn* is one of my favorite books of all time. Slavery has had such a huge impact on American society that issues such as affirmative action, which feels very current, are being affected by it. With friends, I've been known to start shouting over those who don't realize that almost everything that deals with socio-economic factors also deals with racial factors because the two are so tightly linked. As an *individual*, this makes me opinionated. As a *black woman*, this makes me "normal." The stereotype is that blacks are angry and loud, which, if I care enough about the subject, fits me to a tee. This isn't a positive view, though; people assume you're genetically wired to be like this, which makes you less rational than everyone else around you. So, not only do I stand to misinform my classmates on what "the average black person" thinks, but I can be seen as irrational if my opinion exceeds the allotted amount of passion. Now do you see why I never raise my hand?

We also read *The Adventures of Huckleberry Finn* in high school, in a classroom with three black students and two Chinese. We read articles on the book, we studied opinions on it, and we'd make fun of the NAACP's issues with the book constantly; clearly, by calling it offensive, they missed the point. During roundtable discussions in class, the black and Chinese kids would purposely sit away from each other; the joke was that we needed to integrate the room. Sometimes, when our teacher read it aloud, she said the word; other times, she didn't. She never apologized, and no one expected her to. Everyone had an opinion, *their* opinion, and she wasn't afraid to talk about things and get everyone's individual perspective. No one in the classroom was anyone else's tour guide, and everyone had an understanding that people were speaking for themselves.

On some level, I suppose college has introduced me to a new type of diversity. Instead of sitting in classes with Mexicans and Australians (yes, *Australians*), I sit with the suburbanites and rural people I've always secretly feared. My only real experience with those who dwell in the suburbs is the one time my high school mediation team went up to Seneca Valley, a local suburban high school, for "Diversity Day" (we joked for weeks that the title came from the fact that we ourselves were the diversity).

Sitting next to the kid who "never really had any black friends" is a new experience for me, one I should probably cherish. Perhaps he likes whiney white boys with guitars, too, or maybe he's secretly a hip-hop aficionado and, in my ignorance, I missed this. That farm girl in front of me could transcend the idea of the country bumpkin and prove to be politically educated. I could teach this person about my personal experiences, and we could both learn something. Notice I said *personal*. I'm not here to teach anybody about "the black experience." There isn't one, just like there isn't really a "suburban experience," a "female experience," or any other type of experience. For all certain people have in common, whether it be location or race or gender, we are not the same.

I had a conversation once about what it means to be black or white in America. In a John Deere hat and a plaid shirt, the guy I was talking to was the picture of white farm boy. Under normal circumstances, those items alone would be my excuse to get the hell away from him, but I didn't. I'd talked to him before, and although he's what I'm afraid of on the outside, he does something that other people on campus won't: he sees me as a person, a single person. We sat there and had an open conversation about race (he thinks people blow things way out of proportion and do stupid things because of it; I think sometimes we don't take things seriously enough) and guess what? I made a friend! We aren't the same, but we can be honest, and that is the first step.

I'm sure others have been in similar situations. As we were walking down the street from dinner once, a college friend of mine told me that in class that week he was asked for "the gay perspective" on abstinence; he was cracking up the entire time he told me. After leaving a lecture by Maya Angelou (which feels like a very "black" thing to attend), another friend told me that a white classmate came up to her and apologized for her loss because Rosa Parks had died. She had never met Rosa before in her life. Her reaction was one of awe and confusion; *nobody* is really that clueless. None of us ever get upset in front of these people; it's not as if people know any better. The fact that they ask questions at all shows that they aren't being malicious, but rather insanely ignorant. More often than not, I simply avoid questions. I don't want to be "the angry black woman," a stereotype that has caused me to be silent to avoid it. To be honest, though, I'm tired of being quiet. I didn't come to school to be censored, especially by myself. All I ask is that you see me the way I see you: as a person, an individual. Then, perhaps, we can sit back and discuss why slavery is indeed bad.

Sorry

Ashley Birt
Second Place for College Prose, 2007

My older sister is sorry, although you'd never get that just from meeting her. She isn't sad and pathetic sorry, or *I didn't mean to break your window with my baseball* sorry. She's knock you over with her bike and help you up sorry, sit alone in a church because she feels guilty for something that happened ten years ago sorry. She's *I'd help you move into your new apartment, but I have better things to do* sorry, puke on your shoes while drunk sorry, shouldn't have shown those naked baby pictures to your boyfriend sorry. She's not bake you a Bundt cake sorry, not roses say it best sorry. She's steal money from Mom's purse and replace it sorry, *It hurt me more than it hurt you when I hit you* sorry. She's break your Barbies because they're stupid, run away when Mom and Dad find out, get dragged back by the ear sorry. She's hold your hair back while you're vomiting sorry, *I shouldn't have made you eat worms* sorry, *do me a favor and don't die from this* sorry.

She's never wear a dress because she hates them even though it would make Mom happy sorry. She's won't play house with you because the boys are more fun, although she still loves you sorry. She's *hand me that teakettle, we can play now since I knocked out Joseph's teeth by accident* sorry.

She's *it's not my fault Mom and Dad like me better* sorry, *you were an accident and that wasn't my fault* sorry, *I don't control the universe* sorry. *The world expects me to be normal, but I don't know what that is* sorry, *I didn't mean to embarrass you in front of your friends, it's their fault they mistook me for a boy* sorry. *Mom only smiles at you because you keep your hair long and I won't grow mine, but that's because it's my expression of individuality, and if no one else understands it, then they can go to hell, and so can you for not defending me when they tried to lock me in my locker, sometimes I need help, too* sorry, *but I guess you're still too little to know right from wrong.*

She's *I didn't mean to look at your friend like that* sorry, *I promise I didn't mean anything by it, although would it be awful if I said she's kind of hot* sorry. She's *I don't know how to get in touch with my feminine side, Mom, but I'll try for you* sorry. She's short skirt, wobble in heels, fall on her face and hate herself sorry, the whole school just saw her underwear sorry, you want to crawl in a hole and die sorry. She's won't help you with your math homework because Joseph and his two fake teeth asked her out today sorry. She's celebrate getting her license by picking you and your best friend up and taking you out for ice cream sorry, guilty for blowing off Joseph because he's boring and can't handle not wearing the pants in the relationship even though he likes her sorry, make out with your friend in the back seat while you're supposedly in the bathroom and attempt to explain sorry. *We were just playing, I mean it's really nothing, she made me do it* sorry, *I didn't mean to hurt Joseph, it's not him, it's me* sorry, *for the love of God please don't tell Mom and Dad, they'll kill us both.*

She's *I hate to make you keep secrets* sorry, *I hate to ask this, but can you teach me to be girly,* never understand why she prefers boy's clothing but realizes that people ask you about it sorry. She's wrap you up in blankets, feed you chicken soup, sing you to sleep when you're sick, still feels bad about making you eat worms when you were six sorry.

She's *I don't think I'll ever be a proper girl, ever want to be a proper girl, does that bother you* sorry. She's the man at the corner store called her sir and she didn't correct him, which made her feel good, but that's not something to be proud of sorry. She's *give me the sponge* sorry, *they should've written 'dyke' on my locker, not yours, although I suppose what they wrote on mine was worse* sorry, *I'll understand if you won't love me after this, I wouldn't love me, I know Mom and Dad won't* sorry.

She's not send you chocolates for forgetting your birthday sorry or feel guilty for not saying goodbye to her girlfriend before leaving for summer camp sorry, but *oops, did I knock out your teeth again, Joseph* sorry, *you shouldn't have tried to get laid by my sister, I don't care if I wouldn't sleep with you* sorry. She's take karate to kick someone's ass for calling her queer, take karate to kick someone's ass for bothering you because she's queer sorry. She's pay you twenty bucks not to tell Dad she took you to a gay club sorry, pay you twenty more because the DJ called her by her drag name and thought you were her date. She's *you shouldn't have to keep this many secrets* sorry, *don't tell me go to hell for missing your graduation, I had a lot on my mind, I feel awful enough as it is* sorry. She's bury her head in the sand like a loser sorry, feel bad for being jealous since *Mom likes you better now* sorry, *can't get into college and feels stupid for it* sorry.

She's *I hate to ask, but call me Michael, not Michelle, my new girlfriend calls me Michael* sorry, disappear for days and come home drunk and miserable sorry, *I can't believe I ever let people kick my ass behind the bleachers, tell me no one touched you* sorry. She's *I told Dad I was Daddy's little boy, not girl, and he ran me out of the house with a kitchen knife, I don't want to bother you but I need a place to stay* sorry.

She is *didn't mean to make you feel awkward* sorry, *I always embarrassed you* sorry, *I'll be a better person* sorry.

She's afraid to ask but needs you to walk her home for fear of someone trying to kill her sorry, wishes you didn't know all her secrets sorry, wishes she could protect you like you protect her sorry, wishes you loved her like she loves you sorry.

I'm wish I could I say how deep my love runs sorry, how grateful I am and thankful for my older sister, but that would involve admitting to you and to myself that my older sister is now my older brother sorry. I'm able to accept it, able to embrace it, but simply unable to ever say it sorry. I'm the one who's truly sorry.

Dear Dad/Sperm Donor

Rebecca Bortman
Second Place for College Poetry, 2006

My biggest concerns are heart disease and cancer.
Do they run in the family? I kept getting asked
at appointments and I always have to say,
"I am fifty percent unsure."
Once when I was giving blood, the nurse got so excited:
"I have never met anyone like you before."
People always say that.
"Good for your mother. She must be a unique lady."
Thinking Mom was some sort of independent lesbian or
logical single woman blinking menopause.
I didn't have the heart to tell her I had a real dad.

What I really want to know is,
What I am? Am I Irish? Russian? All Polish?
In Scotland, I was, "One of the most American looking
people I have ever seen."
I suppose my face suggests
boring, pale, and prairie state.
Maybe that's just my Polish
half covering up something
wonderful. Some rich heritage
like Native American or Japanese.
My boyfriend Carlos tells me
I dance as well as any Puerto Rican
and I adore the delicacy
of burnt rice at the bottom of the pot.
What I really want to be is Jewish.

Please, please, please. Say I am Jewish.
All the Shabbats and Yom Kippurs
don't stop the mothers from,
"Well, you don't look Jewish."
An Asian boy once saw *the pain of ages*
in my eyes and said he knew I was Jewish.
Whatever I am. Thank you.
Thank you for all limbs and no disease
and a quality brain and acne so I'd use the brain.

Some good did come from filling
that cup after all. Did you know?

It's strange. I knew. I was twelve at a highway
diner and my parents started to tell me,
but I stopped them.
I had only ever heard
about it from watching *Made in America*
with Ted Danson and Whoopi Goldberg.
Hey, am I black?
Until I know for sure, I say, "I might be," to all those
"Are you . . . ?" questions.
It's better that way.
In the diner I stopped them, "I know, I'm adopted."
That was wrong. Then I guessed right.

All I know is that you were a medical
student and likely a doctor by now.
So I hope that's working out for you.

A Crime Too Dark

Brittany Boyd
Second Place for High School Prose, 2004

Many people believe that African Americans receive a great amount of discrimination from Caucasian Americans. Although this is true, there is a growing problem within the African American community itself. That problem is lighter colored vs. darker colored. This mindset, that light is closest to white must be right and if you are darker skinned then you are held to lower standards, has made itself relevant to almost every African American. Unfortunately, I have experienced this discrimination firsthand.

Fourth grade was a year of fun and friendships, little boys chasing little girls around the room, and trying to find out more about your childhood life. There were laughs, tears, and so many other emotions. I went to a predominantly African American elementary school called John Morrow, so I had more experience with different cultures, whereas most of the kids in my school had gone to St. Benedict since kindergarten. Therefore, they did not converse with many cultures outside of the African American one.

One day while outside at recess, the boys and girls were chasing one another, as usual. There was this one little boy whom I had the biggest crush on. I told my friend at the time that I like him so much and I would love to be his fourth-grade girlfriend. So while everyone was running around, my friend went over to him and said, "Who do you wanna go with? Chanel or Brittany?"

In response he said, "Chanel because she is light and Brittany is too black."

It was then that I had my first experience with black-on-black racism.

I am not a dark-skinned girl, maybe medium. However, his words affected me so much that from fourth grade to eighth grade, I thought that all light brown people were prettier than dark brown people. I would look through magazines and say, "Eww . . . look at that dark girl! She is so ugly!"

It wasn't until one day when I was conversing with my mom that I realized this feeling that I had was wrong and racist. I explained to my mother that I thought she was a lot prettier than me because of her lighter skin. My mother then made me look in the mirror and tell her what I saw.

Well, I said, "I see my face."

"And what is it that you like most about your face?" my mother asked.

"My smile!" I said. "I think that I have an okay smile."

"Okay then. It doesn't matter how dark your skin is or how light your skin is. We are all beautiful. We all have different things about ourselves that we like," my mother said.

After hearing these words from my mom, I realized that I was being silly for saying that lighter colored people were far prettier than medium- or darker-colored people.

I was one of the many African Americans who have been led astray to think that black-on-black racism was okay. For me, it was my peers in fourth grade that had influenced my thinking. For many now it is the media. The media plays such a big role in differentiating between the darker-skinned people and the lighter-skinned people. I was watching a TV show one day about being against your own race. There was an African American lady on the show, and she was just going on and on about how ugly darker-skinned people were and how she is so blessed to be light skinned. It sickened me to see a grown lady talking about this black-on-black racism. However, I could not blame her—she later explained that when she was younger, her mother would tell her to stay away from the darker kids because they would mess up her reputation. She was led astray, just as other African Americans often are.

Many think that this feeling of discrimination within our own race goes all the way back to slavery when it was thought that those whose color was lighter than a brown paper bag had the chance of "passing" as white, if given the opportunity. And those who were lighter were able to work in the house, instead of in the field, and were usually treated with more respect there. This feeling of resentment has continued to infect the African American community through generations and generations.

How can we even try to fight off discrimination from Caucasians when we are having so much discrimination between ourselves? Martin Luther King urged us to learn to respect and love ourselves before we can expect others to respect us. I believe that the African American community must learn to fight this black-on-black racism before it diminishes the dignity of further generations.

Another Challenge to the Dream

Brittany Boyd
Honorable Mention for High School Prose, 2005

When I read the email that I had won second place in Carnegie Mellon University's Martin Luther King, Jr. Day writing contest last year, I felt very proud of my accomplishment. In addition to winning second place, my article was also featured in the *Pittsburgh Post-Gazette* newspaper on Martin Luther King's birthday. I was excited that my story had been recognized as a good piece of writing, and I was even more excited because I knew that I would be able to speak in a university setting. This honor meant that my concern about black-on-black racism would be heard at a respectable college. When I took my place at the podium, my heart was beating fast and my palms were sweaty; however, I also felt a sense of great pride to be able to present my story. I was sharing an important message of the need to stop black-on-black racism.

Shortly after the contest while I was at school, a message appeared on the message board addressed to me. I wondered who would be sending me mail at school. My friend Na-Tasha and I went into the bathroom so that I could read the letter in private. When I opened the letter, I saw that it was regarding the essay I had written for the contest. Immediately I thought to myself that it must be a letter congratulating me on how much they liked my essay since it was featured in the *Post-Gazette*. However, the more I read the letter, the more that I saw that it was quite the opposite.

The "stranger" who wrote the letter to me identified himself by an address label that had a picture of General Robert E. Lee on it. In addition, a Confederate flag had been copied on the right side of the paper. It never occurred to me that the letter that I had received would be one that would cause me fear, nervousness, and a deeper understanding of racism.

In the opening of his letter he wrote, "I dispute the common black claim of white discrimination against you people" —an objection that confused me because my essay focused on black-on-black racism. His letter also included other provocative statements such as, "I don't call it discrimination for us whites to take reasonable self-protective steps to protect ourselves against black violence and black crime," and, "You blacks run your mouth and the white power structure caters to you blacks and gives you blacks whatever you demand."

As I read the letter over and over again in my school's bathroom, I grew more and more angry and fearful of this man. Tears began to build up in my eyes, yet I was too embarrassed to let my black friend Na-Tasha see me cry. I was confused. First, why did this man write such crude remarks to me? I was only in eleventh grade. Second, why were his words so hurtful and racist? For the first time in my life, I did not feel like a human being; I felt like an animal.

Being referred to as "you blacks" with such negative connotations stirred up feelings of anger in me. I was hurt and embarrassed.

Finally, I let Na-Tasha read the letter, and then when she was done, I had to leave to catch my bus. As I walked out of my school's doors, tears rolled down my face. During the bus ride home, I couldn't help but read the letter over and over again. When I got home, I ran into my mom's arms and showed her the letter. The tears were uncontrollable at that point, and I was entirely distressed. My mom immediately tried to soothe me with her tender words, as she always does when I am upset. She told me to try not to focus on this man's words. From the tone of his letter, she said, he appeared bitter and there was nothing we could do to change his feelings. She then reminded me that only I could control how I reacted to his letter.

I have many friends from various races and I have always felt accepted. However, amidst the diversity within my group of friends, I finally realized that some people still believe in the white supremacy and Jim Crow racist laws. All of my life, I have strived to live by Martin Luther King's lead and not react violently or crudely when racist slurs or thoughts have been said to me. Even though I had gotten this rude letter from this man, my values did not have to budge nor change. I would continue to lead a good life and be an example for others. I did not react rudely to the letter.

From this experience, I realized how humiliating an attack of verbally degrading and vulgar words can make anyone feel whether you are white, black, man, or woman. However, it is an individual's choice how he or she will react to the situation. I truly believe that this concept of maintaining individual integrity is the message that Martin Luther King, Jr. wrote of and displayed. Yes, he was called every name in the book, imprisoned, and sought out to be killed. However, rather than reacting with violence, he reacted with tolerance and intelligence.

Being a Minority in a School of the White and Privileged

Djibril Branche
First Place for High School Prose, 2017

A Step-by-Step Guide

Step One: Your Name
Remember the proud dignity that was once your name? Remember that even the phrase "proud dignity" itself is a teeny-weeny bit challenging to pronounce, and even more difficult to spell; so when it comes to the proud dignity of your actual name, expect some alterations when you first announce it to your peers. Usually, in order that your name becomes palatable for even the simplest of speakers, the alteration will arrive in the form of a shortening, but in special cases, if your name is versatile enough, be prepared for many renditions. For example, if your name is Djibril, one can expect names like "Stabril," "Djibo," "Jipy," and maybe even "Jigaboo." Be sure to laugh along with the other kids. ALWAYS LAUGH ALONG WITH THE OTHER KIDS, because you want to make a good first impression. Also, be sure to recognize that the beautiful cascade of sounds that is—or should I say was—your name is now whatever your class considers its most hilarious perversion. Your name has now become entertainment with its new purpose to amuse rather than to manifest your individuality. Don't expect the hilarity to go away anytime soon; you're stuck with it, of course you would be, it's your name after all.

Step Two: "Where are you from?"
Now depending on your hue, some people at your school—students, faculty, administrators, and staff—might anticipate a certain exoticism to your birthplace and a simple "Hartford, Connecticut" just won't do. As if attempting to wring some sort of secret artifact out of you, the dissatisfied will ask again, and again, and again putting increasing stress on the word "from" each time. Suggestion: don't think of the question as "where are you from?" Think of it more as "What makes you the other, a minority?" OR "if your people hadn't been kidnapped and enslaved, and if records had been kept, try to imagine what your nationality would be if you were to look at a contemporary map of the world." Try your best to satisfy the inquisitive asker to that end.

Step Three: Racial Humor
A significant element of presenting as black in a majority white school is the categorization of every single attempt at racial humor that uninvitingly lands on your doorstep as "funny" and "harmless." These pitiful excuses for comedy rarely deviate from the classic "Haha, you're (insert race here)" format. However, the five iterations of this same joke can and will occur in a multitude of situations: being late to class might inspire the quip, "He was on his own CPT (colored people time)"; the act of running might inspire, "He's so fast because he's used to running from the

cops." IF the word "black" is introduced in literally any context while you're in the room, the environment will become slightly darker than usual. No matter how much you may protest, your race and all the struggles inherent therein will be reduced to the mere punchline of a joke. Always be sure to laugh at EVERY. SINGLE. ONE. You don't want to be seen as oversensitive and as someone that can't take a joke, do you? And besides, laughing is often—not always but often—way better than the alternative, in which you're forced to believe someone was attempting to perpetuate America's oldest and most horrific tradition. So you laugh and hope it's the last time you have to hear it.

It never is.

Lastly, a short list of banned foods:
Chicken (especially fried)
Watermelon
Kool-Aid (or any drink that resembles Kool-Aid, so particularly opaque brands of fruit punch are also out)

Remembering and applying what you learned here should make your school experience bearable, painless even! Just know that you will need to remember these steps throughout elementary, middle, and if you're really unlucky, high school. But do be careful when going out into the world, 'cause there's a whole different set of rules for that one.

Microagression

Irina Bucur
Third Place for High School Poetry, 2016

1.
Honey, can you translate for your mother?

2.
I'm not sure she understands.

3.
Granola. Gra-no-la bar.

4.
It would be a good thing to learn those words in English.

5.
Do they not use birth control in your culture?

6.
You're from Russia, or wherever?

7.
Same thing.

8.
It must have been tough for your parents.

9.
Are you Communist?

10.
But you're legal, right?

11.
No offense.

12.
You know, we're in America. Things are done differently here.

American Jeans

Connie Chan
Third Place for College Prose, 2013

Kindergarten—1997
In Marysville Elementary School's cafeteria, I stared at the unfamiliar, layered food item in front of me: a tan, domed piece of bread atop a slice of slippery pink meat, a perfect square of vibrant yellow cheese, and another piece of bread (except this one was flat). That day's lunch menu read, "turkey sandwich."

The simple entrée was exotic compared to the foods I was used to in San Jose, California, my birthplace and home until my parents decided to load up our 1992 Honda Civic and migrate to Dorothy's land—Marysville, Kansas, to be exact.

I looked around at the other kids, trying to gauge how to eat my food. Most grabbed this "sandwich" by two hands, with their thumbs on the bottom and other fingers digging into the top. They passed around a red bottle and a yellow bottle, squirting large globs of sauce on the turkey. Some were more creative and traced designs onto the edible canvas. By the time they were done, the sauce fell over the sides of the sandwich, plopping on their food trays like paint on a palette.

American cuisine was still quite foreign to me, growing up in my parent's yet-to-be-assimilated home, which smelled of ginger and sesame oil rather than vanilla and butter. I immersed myself in American culture the only way I knew how: through imitation. Assuming my neighbor's condiment waterfall was the typical portion, I placed a generous dollop of red in the center of my sandwich, topped by another heavy dollop of yellow.

The lunch lady on duty saw our well-dressed sandwiches and frowned in disapproval. "Don't play with your food," she said. Play? Several of my peers giggled at their exploited sandwiches, which they never planned on eating; the sandwiches were nothing more than amusement for kindergarten children. I had been duped. Embarrassed at my misunderstanding of their entertainment as normalcy, I pushed down on the spongy top bread to hide my sauce of shame. I ended up throwing my sandwich away without ever taking a bite.

Second Grade—1999
Marysville High School was hosting its annual field day for the local elementary students as well as those from a few neighboring towns. The high school's signature red track and field area had been transformed into stations for tire-rolling contests, Frisbee tosses, and many other simple athletic games. After the adult volunteers blew their whistles, I rotated to my next station—the potato sack race. The children lined up behind the burlap sacks that lay on the scratchy grass. One by one, clumsy children took turns crawling into the stiff sacks to participate in this strange game of handicapped hop-frog. The race progressed at a slow and sloppy rate, so the children waiting in line had time to kill. I was familiar with most of the kids that surrounded me, except for a few from Beattie, which was a 15-minute drive from Marysville. From a short distance across the football field, two of the Beattie girls stared at

me. I wasn't compelled to say anything because I hated breaking the comfortable silence that always surrounded me. I figured if I didn't interact with my peers, then negative interaction was impossible. Besides, my aunt always told me, "Do not talk if unnecessary" —and from what I had heard over the years from my classmates, almost everything was unnecessary. As a result, my quiet personality made me difficult to approach and easy to overlook.

Yet for some reason, the girls decided to look at me, of all things, on that eventful day. Once I made eye contact with the shorter one, she taunted me.

"Chinese girl can't jump!" she giggled, which prompted her second-in-command to laugh as well. Though they were just two girls—neither taller than a miniature Christmas tree—I felt like they had great power over me. They initiated an attack, and the best I could hope for was a good defense. But I said nothing. The comment came and went, and whistles and joyful whoops from the field drowned out the girl's comment. The expression on her face did not reflect the severity of what she had just said. It was nothing to her; she continued to kick up dirt from the field. I was numb.

When I thought the humiliating experience was over after a matter of seconds, a blond boy in my class piped up.

"She can jump!" I turned around to face David. He looked at me with eyes like gleaming blue marbles and gave me a sweet smile. "You can do it, Connie."

Though I wasn't particularly close to David at the time, I felt safer. He had the reputation of being a smart aleck, but he could be a sweetheart nonetheless.

Even to David's kind words, I said nothing. I thanked him the only way I knew how: I potato-sacked. Not wanting to let David down, I hopped as hard as gravity would let me. With each bound across the field, I felt the burlap sack taut across the bottom of my shoes—a force that both stunted my stride and pulled me up off the ground, kind of like the mix of peers I left behind as I leapt across the finish line.

Fourth Grade—2001

Tiffany had sparse mousy hair the color of dirty parchment. Her face was sunken in and lacked the jovial youth of most fourth graders. Tiffany's uniformly dull skin stretched over her rigid features and begged for a splash of color—even her lips were only half a shade darker, a muted brown. But if I had the choice, I would rather look at Tiffany than talk to her. My conversations with Tiffany were never stimulating; we chatted while waiting in line at the water fountain or in the few minutes before recess was over. Day after day, I would have to pretend to be stumped by the dense questions she posed. But I gave Tiffany some credit; she at least noticed that I looked different from everyone else—which prompted her to ask me if I could speak Spanish.

But one day, Tiffany's curious personality caught me off guard. Staring between my eyes, Tiffany pinched the bridge of her own nose and said, "Why is right here so short?"

I remembered feeling an uncomfortable surge of heat to my head. Why did she have to ask me why I looked different? It was like asking why her hair was lighter than mine or why she was taller than me. That's just how things were. My fourth-grade self wished to be more educated at the time, to express my annoyance and frustration in a respectable way. Even so, I wasn't about to synthesize the concept of genetics to some nincompoop like Tiffany. There was too much anger in me that couldn't be settled, but I only replied, "I don't know."

Looking back, I knew it was an innocent question on Tiffany's part. My rage was fueled by her direct address to something I didn't want to acknowledge: I looked drastically different from everyone else. That day, I surreptitiously stared at the noses of all my classmates. Sure enough, they all had nice and tall bridges, like skyscrapers or the Statue of Liberty; this is what America looked like—not like me. My eyes were the shape of sunflower seeds and my strands of strikingly dark hair fell in small locks across my face like dangling vanilla beans. My classmates had light and fluffy hair, blinding in the sun. My skin had a sharp yellow tint that contrasted with their peachy hues. I stood out like a stain on white sheets. Luckily, I was half a head shorter than most my peers, and that was the only way I could be lost in a crowd.

Fifth Grade—2002

As a child, I always hated shopping with my mom. She liked to dress me in pretty patterns and monochromatic outfit sets, reminiscent of vibrant Chinese opera costumes. Though the darling getup and glittery butterfly hairpins drew compliments from my teachers, the dresses and skirts were impractical for a tomboy and inhibited full play during recess. I was paranoid the wind would catch my velvet bejeweled skirt while I ran or swung on the monkey bars, so on those days, I sat on the shallow curb by the basketball hoops. I watched my classmates run around in their Nike shorts, blue jeans, and T-shirts from summer camps and sports clinics. I always admired the casual attire of the "jocks." Even if they weren't actually good at sports, I assumed they were skilled because they looked the part. Only a true athlete had the right to walk around in that uniform.

I would have been grateful for the small downgrade to jeans: my legs had never touched denim until the fifth grade. I had asked my mom for jeans before, but she claimed cotton pants and leggings were better because they stretched and easily fit my petite Asian frame. But in fifth grade—by some hand-me-down miracle or lapse in judgment on my mother's part—I received my first pair of jeans. It felt like a rite of passage, though they were not the least bit flattering: baggy, straight-legged, and a few inches short. I paired it with a gray T-shirt sponsored by our local bank that read "think big, be big" in bold black lettering on the front; the back was tattooed with logos of other local businesses. These two frumpy articles of clothing constituted my favorite outfit, to the disgust of my mom. I didn't look as adorable as my pastel legging-clad self or adorable at all for that matter. I looked like an all-American, run-of-the-mill kid—and that's exactly what I liked about it.

On my first day of sporting the jeans, I received many comments about how I looked older, yet nobody could figure out why. It was the first day that I was not my mother's dress-up doll, not adorned with fruity velvet vests or pants with intricate stitching. I played dumb about the comments, refusing to point out my first pair of jeans—a milestone everyone else had reached years ago. It was curious how the faded blue jeans, which were identical to everyone else's, attracted more attention than my old wardrobe. I stood out more when I tried to look like everyone else.

Lost Heritage

Brianna Kline Costa
Honorable Mention for High School Poetry, 2016

Blue eyes,
light skin,
pink cheeks,
thin lips,
freckles strewn across a face like stars,
yet to form constellations.

I do not look like the photos in
my Spanish textbook.

I wear a mask, accompanied
by the advantage of privilege,
yet it leaves me tied to the guilt
of abandoning an ethnicity that abandoned
me in Santa Fe, New Mexico,
eight months before I was born.

~

My name is a simple name.
My name is a common name.
My name is a teacher-pronounces-it-right-the first-time-
during-attendance name,
a souvenir shop keychain name.

I hate it.

I don't want a name that is easy to spell
or easy to remember.
I want a name that's exotic,
I want a name that drips from your tongue
like honey, that rings in the air like a chorus of trumpets.

Esperanza.
Maria.
Catalina.

I want a name to tell the secret
which my appearance disguises

and which my lips can never
seem to form.

~

I don't know what to do with this part of me.
I don't know where to keep it.
Perhaps I will loop its tendrils
around my rib cage where it will be safe,
or paint the letters on my wrist for all to see.

I have never been scared to claim something
that it is my own.
I've never been one to let people
take something that is mine,
or to abandon something
that I have.

But I don't know if I can claim this.

I don't know if it is mine to claim.

Untitled

Shane Creepingbear
Second Place for High School Poetry, 2001

When I was young,
There were no other races than red.
Not red skin,
But redneck.
I grew up in Small Town, Ohio (right by the lake).
In second grade there was a black girl.
The only black girl in Small Town.
In second grade I would watch kids call her
Monkey and
Nigger.
In second grade, I did not know what those words meant.
I knew I wasn't black, but
In second grade I didn't know I wasn't white.

Nobody asked, but
I knew I wasn't black.
One teacher treated me differently
Than the other kids in Small Town.
Once I was sent into the hall for sneezing too loud,
Once I had to sit in the hall for not bringing the "right"
Crayons to school.

No one asked if I wanted to play.
At recess I sat alone.
I would swing on the swings,
See how tall I could make a pile of rocks.
But I couldn't play football, or tag.
I was never asked to.
I didn't care, they never teased me.
The teachers never asked me questions.
Neither did the kids.

When I finally found out I was never going to turn white
I was confused, though excited.
I'm an Indian, I told people.
They were fascinated.

Now they asked me how to hunt and make tomahawks.

The "S" Word

Kristen Deasy
Third Place for High School Prose, 2017

Growing up, we are all taught words that we shouldn't say. We hear them on TV, in movies, or from adults around us. Some of these words make others uncomfortable, so we are told not to repeat them. As children, we have to know why we aren't allowed to do or say something, but sometimes we are not given a clear answer. As a result, we live our whole lives with a subconscious negative meaning attached to these words. The most common one we all know is probably the "s word." The word isn't shit, but suicide.

I can't recall the first time I heard the word suicide, but I can remember at a young age being confused about what it was and never having it explained to me. Anytime I heard the word or spoke the word "suicide" there was an automatic tension in the room, one I didn't understand. In grade school, there was a story on the news about a man who committed suicide by jumping off a bridge near my house. I felt sad, but I was also cynical towards the man. That sounds weird because I never knew him, but I thought that killing himself was selfish. I thought about his family, his friends, all of the lives he was affecting by taking his own. I didn't understand at the time that the man was sick and that his illness had prompted him to act. When I asked questions about the incident, everyone stayed silent, which added to the weird tension around the word.

When I was in seventh grade, there was a shooting at Western Psychiatric Hospital. This was the first time I learned that Pittsburgh, the city I've lived in since birth, has a psychiatric hospital. I live less than ten miles away from this hospital and had no idea it existed. After hearing about the shooting and watching it consume the news, I assumed this hospital served crazy people. I had heard of psychiatric hospitals prior to this and anytime they were talked about it was in a negative way. I used the terms "nut house," "insane asylum" and "psycho" to describe the hospital and those inside of it, not realizing that it's a serious hospital helping people who are legitimately sick. In a society where everything we say has to be "politically correct," it's ironic that I was never corrected when using those terms, words that were not appropriate to be using.

As the hysteria around the shooting slowly ended, I didn't think much about the hospital or the types of people within it. The only time I ever thought about mental health was when I saw antidepressant commercials on TV. The commercials always showed an adult who couldn't get out of bed because they were "so sad." These overdramatic commercials irritated me more than a commercial should. I didn't believe that these people were as sad as the commercial made them seem. "Life isn't that miserable," I thought to myself. I was skeptical that a pill could make someone happy, and the plethora of side effects rambled off at the end of the commercial really didn't convince me. I thought that people who needed an antidepressant were just exaggerating their symptoms of sadness. Little did I know, I would become one of the people from the commercial. I had been applying stereotypes and discriminating against people with mental illness for years, when in reality I was one of those people.

For years I had denied my symptoms of depression for the same reason I didn't believe the commercials: I thought that I was being dramatic. I thought that isolation, skipping meals, and panic attacks were normal for a teenage girl. I was wrong. I put on a mask for years, pretending to be happy, just so people didn't label me as "the attention-seeking one." The mask was exhausting to wear 24/7, so sometimes my family could tell something was wrong. When they suggested I see a therapist, I said that there was absolutely no way I was seeing a shrink. "I'm not crazy," I told them. I was so offended that they thought I was the type of person who needed to see a psychiatrist. When they pushed the topic, I argued that they were overreacting, that I was just being a normal teenage girl. But what does any of that mean? The word "crazy" or "the type of person who needs to see a psychiatrist?" Why did I think that it's wrong if someone needs to see a therapist? Why was I offended when my parents suggested I talk to someone? Why was I discriminating against myself?

My mindset was completely transformed while in the waiting room of the hospital that I once thought crazy people went to: Western Psych. I had previously visited the hospital a few months earlier after a severe panic attack, but even after that visit, I didn't accept that I was sick. This time was different though; I had actually tried to take my own life. So many things entered my mind in the waiting room this time around. I thought of how I viewed mental illness: how I thought people who went to psychiatric hospitals were crazy; that people on antidepressant commercials were dramatic; that people who committed or attempted suicide were attention seeking. I applied all of these labels to myself. I realized I was one of the "crazy, dramatic, attention-seeking" people. This realization came to me after my dad told me something in the waiting room that I remind myself of every day. He said, "Kristen, if you had a broken foot we would take you to the hospital to get it fixed. There is something wrong with your brain so we are going to get that fixed." He couldn't have been more right. We are so quick to treat something like a broken foot or diabetes, but when we can't see exactly what's wrong, we ignore it. I thought to myself, "Our brains are the most important part of the body, yet we give it the least attention. If our brain isn't working properly, how can the rest of our body?" This thought made me angry. I was angry because I used to judge and discriminate against people who were seriously ill. I was angry because I knew most of society has the same mindset I used to have. I was angry because we don't talk about mental illness and we don't try and educate people about what it really is. I was angry that the word "suicide" makes people uncomfortable, and so we ignore it. I was angry at how big of a problem this is.

During the months following my hospitalization, I slowly recovered and became more aware of how severe the discrimination against mental illness is. Because I missed school to recover and receive treatment, I didn't hear the rumors floating around the halls about why I was absent. I eventually started to get word that people were saying I was a "psychopath" and "faking it." I tried to ignore the rumors, but deep down it hurt. I had no desire to return to school because I dreaded seeing the people who were saying these things about me. Once I returned, though, the worst part weren't the rumors or the mean names; it was the way people isolated me. Girls who I had gone to school with acted like I was a completely different person; they were afraid to talk to me, afraid of saying or doing the wrong things. I was awkwardly approached and was treated like I had been living on Mars for five years. I was so bothered. I didn't want my classmates to think of me any differently just because I had a sickness. I know for some of them it was pure shock. I had always appeared to be an extremely outgoing, confident person, so the news of me trying to kill myself was a slap in the face for most. I tried to ignore it and surround myself with people who didn't treat me differently for what I had gone through. But I was still bothered. Not because I was offended, but bothered because people thought they had to treat me differently. But I thought to myself, five years ago I probably would have treated someone with a mental illness the same way I was treated, with fear and judgment. I could have accepted the treatment I received, but I couldn't just passively let this go on. I wanted to change the attitude around this subject.

I began to talk openly about my battle with depression, and before I knew it, people were reaching out to me for help. This has motivated me to apply what I have learned from my own struggles when encouraging others to ask for help and receive the treatment they deserve and so desperately need. We have created a society that ostracizes people who have invisible illnesses. We live in a world where using every swear word possible in a rap song is appropriate but a word that describes how someone died is not. We need to stop silencing people when the conversation of mental illness is brought up, and we need to start saying the words that make people cringe until they aren't cringeworthy anymore. Because if you had a broken foot, we would get that fixed.

Midnight, Pittsburgh

Terence Degnan
Honorable Mention for College Poetry, 2002

54C south from oakland to downtown
the windows were glossed like a black
and white baseball game where the players'
last names meant their ethnicity
she was a pair of headphones
she had braids pulling all the way back to her roots
and my roots:
i wanted the name adam
i wanted to reach back
to where my family tree ruined us
choke the roots
i don't know my people
my people are dying for potatoes
she was schooling me about the right ways and the
wrong ways my bus would hopscotch
"just wait by the theater
it's my route too"
i could hear the Roots coming through her head
to the good ear she was using to see if i would talk
i would never tell her they were my new pacemaker too
i wanted to look like glass
pure silver
i wanted mercury for blood
and hip-hop lyrics for an epitaph
for every thing wrong happening under stainless steel
white collar chatterboxes
waning above like threats; i wanted blood
i wanted to emit sadness
i was off the bus
melting through every manhole
sending signals across the street for anyone tuned to
hear sobs
for an audience
so i could remain here
i wanted a membership card for this moment
i wanted to find the correct blue
sign to stand in front of and wait forever

Your Stereotypical Biracial Child

Phallon Depante
Honorable Mention for High School Prose, 2008

I am what our society considers to be a biracial person, yet, this being said, when I am asked on the SATs to check the box that best describes my ethnic background, I always put "other." I could check Caucasian, because I am majority white, but by doing that I would be denying my African American background. My dad's mother always told him that biracial children are just "niggers with lighter skin." Growing up, I was always baffled as to why when I went to my dad's parent's apartment they would leave the room and never talk to me. To my naïve six-year-old mind I looked just like them, but with maturity came the knowledge of the one-drop rule. Even though I looked just like my dad, was ghostly pale and with all the trimmings of a perfect little Italian girl, I was still some other little "nigger" child because my mother had given me her black blood. My dad's mom had told him that I would never amount to anything and that I would be "another nigger walkin' the streets beggin' for money."

After hearing things like this said right in front of me, I realized why my mother didn't allow me to see my dad's family that often. So I grew up with my mom's African American family.

My grandmother has been such a huge part of my life. The majority of my childhood was me spending time with her, watching her cook, listening to her sing and joke around with the other members of my family. Although I was content with the relationship I had with my mom's family, I still wondered why my dad's family couldn't accept and love me the same way. Once while I was in the store with my grandmother, she ran into one of her friends from "down the bottom," as she would call it. I was standing there listening to them reminisce and catch up on the latest gossip, and then the woman focused her attention on me. She spoke to me and then I asked my grandmother if she was babysitting me. My grandmother explained that I was "Chloe's daughter by some white man," all the while playing with my then-long hair. The women then proceeded to play with my hair and tell me how beautiful I was. The whole situation was strange to me, and I never understood why she was so fascinated with my hair. My grandmother had such a proud look on her face the entire time, and as they continued to talk about me, grandmother stated that I was "the family's porcelain prize." As time passed, I came to understand why I was considered the "favorite" grandchild.

My African American family, especially my grandmother, was so fixated on skin color and hair texture and length. Although my family was proud of their African American heritage, they still had the mentality of white features being better. My mother was no better. In the spring of 2005 I began to stop eating and developed anorexia. My mother hadn't noticed, maybe because she was in denial, but when she finally found out, she was appalled. Not because I was mentally and physically deteriorating, but because, as she had stated, "Black girls don't get eating disorders, that a white girl thing."

I was confused as to how a disorder had a color. My mother has always done her best with me, she has put me through private schools since fourth grade, given me all of my necessities and more, but I know why she did it. Not only because she has my best interest at heart, but also because she wants me to be able to pass as white. My mother would always brag about my friends, and how they live in Squirrel Hill and Fox Chapel. I am very thankful for all of the opportunities that my mother has given me, but when I first entered private school in fourth grade, I was uncomfortable. Immediately when the other children saw my mother, they began to question me about my race and say little things with Southern accents, as though I were the stereotype of an African American and that was the only way I could understand what they were saying. I felt lost and confused—I didn't understand how to act. When I came to high school, no one questioned my ethnicity, nor did they seem to care, but I dreaded the day when the question as to what I was was raised. The other African Americans at my school somehow knew that I was biracial; I guess "we" have a certain look. When the other kids found out, some were shocked, but most didn't even address it. I was relieved, but then the other African American children began to harass me about why I act so "white," and why I didn't sit with them at lunch. I didn't want to sit at the black table because I didn't want to reinforce segregation. I didn't know how to act black or white. I've always strived to remain true to myself, whatever race others consider me to be. I'm Phallon Depante, and I am your stereotypical biracial child.

My Father Tries to Bond with Me

Jonathan deVries
First Place for College Poetry, 2005 (Tie)

On the winter day
I get home from Mexico,
Dad tries to talk to me.

"You might want
to call up the docks.
Ron will put you to work."

My knees squeeze
in the small passenger seat
of Dad's red pickup
which smells like grease.
The truck almost slides off
our icy driveway's first hill.

"Ya gotta work, son.
Look at where
blacks and Hispanics
are in this world—
they don't want to work.
When I was in Nigeria,
I couldn't play golf
because the course
was used as grazing lands.
A beautiful course with
goats and sheep
shitting everywhere.
I couldn't even play a little golf."

His pickup skids
around a snowy turn.

"I asked a Brit in Nigeria—
that reminds me
have you ever heard a black
say 'ask?'
They can't say 'ask.' They say 'axe.'
I said to the Brit in Nigeria,
'since the Brits pulled out,

has anything gotten better?'
'Not one thing!' he says to me."
On the last hill
the truck's tires spin
like game-show wheels.
We get out and lean into the vehicle.

"Mexicans take siestas—
not working because of the heat?
Huh! Do Americans
take siestas during the summer?"

The truck can't crawl up—
Dad leaves it swung sideways.

"Of course your mother
doesn't want to believe me.
Your mother, the eternal optimist.
Just something for you to think about, son.
Welcome home."

His bloodshot blue,
sixty-six-year-old eyes
water above his gray beard,
tattered like a newspaper
blown around dirty streets.
I walk across
the crunching frozen ground,
look at the house
with the Christmas tree
glaring through the windows,
and wonder whose home this is.

Being Mexican-American Post-Election

Melanie Diaz
First Place for High College Prose, 2017

Day One

Why weren't we enough? It's the day after the election and this is all I can think. I keep thinking back to my grandma, wondering what she would say if she were still alive. I keep wondering if she would think her journey to the United States was worth it after seeing Donald Trump being announced President-Elect. How would she feel seeing a man who labeled Mexican immigrants like herself as "drug dealers, murderers, and rapists" become president of this nation she fled to for safety? And how would she feel knowing that this man also condoned grabbing women by the pussy, when she herself fled from an abusive husband, seeking refuge in the United States, a place where she thought things like that weren't tolerated.

Next, I think of my mother, a woman who truly believes in the American dream of meritocracy, a woman who believes the work she produces speaks louder than the color of her skin, a woman who believes anyone can make it in this nation if you just work hard enough. And I wonder how my mother would cope with Trump's victory, which shattered her American Dream, which stated that her brown skin actually was her defining characteristic, not the twenty-five years of military service, not her three tours of duty, not her twenty years of teaching, but her skin color. Because this day marked the day that 60.5 million people said, "You can sacrifice all you want for this country, but at the end of the day you're still just a Mexican and you are not wanted here."

Finally, I think of my younger sister. I think of the little girl back home who has been trying to erase the color of her skin for her whole fifteen years of existence. I try to think of ways I can explain away the nation's reinforcement of her already-present shame of being "not white enough." I think about how much I'd worked to protect her my whole life, how I took a year off college during my mom's last deployment, how I tried to shelter her from her own self-doubt, and how none of this is enough now. Because far too many people in this country just let her down, just told her that her safety, her rights, and her value weren't enough to stop them from voting for a man that ran a campaign in opposition to her very right to existence.

And when I can't think anymore, I cry. I let my whole body shake as I ask again, *Why weren't we enough? Why didn't they worry about us, the people of color who have been sacrificing for this country generation after generation? And if what we've sacrificed isn't yet enough, then when will it be? How many rivers must we cross, how many battles must we fight, and how much of ourselves must we give up before we become "white enough" to matter?*

Day Two

"How are you today?" asks my white, history professor.

"Pretty bad. I spent most of yesterday in the resource advising center crying with fellow students of color and watching my supervisors break down as well," I reply.

"Really? Your advisors were breaking down? I don't understand that. I just don't get why this election is so emotionally charged. I mean, don't people understand that this was a problem of economics?"

Silence.

How could this professor really not understand why this election is so emotionally charged? Is she really telling me that she didn't experience the same fear that I did throughout this past year? That she didn't hear the same racial slurs, didn't see the hate crimes, didn't fear for herself and her loved ones, not even once? God, how I envy that privilege.

"Professor, everything about this is sexist. Everything about this is racist. Because even if Trump voters didn't intend to oppress us—as women, as people of color—they've legitimized the very rhetoric of sexism and racism and that legitimization will have an impact. And we can't just ignore that impact just because someone wanted an extra dollar because that extra dollar isn't worth sacrificing someone else's rights or someone else's safety."

"Well, we are going to have to understand their point of view if we want to work together."

"Okay."

Fast forward to the end of my film class when another student claims that working together is our only option.

I say, "You're asking me to understand and empathize with people who never understood or acknowledged my existence and what their decision would mean for that existence. You're really asking too much of me right now. And work together? I wish I could, but I'm not sure I can ever heal the tear they've created in my spirit, in my faith. You see, on that night, they stole something from me, something you shouldn't be able to steal from a person. They took my faith, they took my value—two things I never thought to be so fragile and so out of my control. They reminded me that as a woman I have no value here, that as a Mexican-American I have no value here. And with that, they stole the faith I had left for this nation. So, you tell me, how could we ever work together again?"

And as I sobbed for the hundredth time in 48 hours, my white, male professor came to my aid, repeating, "You matter, you are of value, you are important." And I cried more as I realized that just as a white male had taken away my value, a white male was giving it back. Why couldn't it come from me like it came from them? Why didn't I have that same power to save myself? And I let the shame swallow me whole.

Day Three

I look at my little sister's picture, and it's one of the ones with her smiling. It's a photo of the day she and my mom dropped me off at college. She had her short hair then from donating the rest of it to cancer patients, but her smile is still exactly the same. During the election, she said she was ready to go to Canada. What was I supposed to tell her? What was I going to tell a little girl who's been trying to escape the limitation of her brown skin all her life? How could I repair the damage Trump's victory caused and the devaluation of her existence that came with it? How could I help her understand if I didn't understand myself? And how could I help fix her spirit when mine was so badly torn as well?

But my whole life has been about this little girl, about her empowerment, about her protection, about loving her. And if I was tired before, I'm going to be exhausted now. But I'll be damned if I give up fighting now. Because her face, her smile, her spirit is worth fighting for, and I won't stop until every single person in this nation realizes she matters in every decision they make. And once they do, I'll be sure never to let them forget it again. **Because she matters. I matter. We matter.**

And tonight I don't cry.

The Wrath of Hamtaro

Kathleen Dillon
Honorable Mention for High School Poetry, 2004

"Faggot!" the group of kids yelled at us.
We tried to ignore them,
but when standing in lines,
you feel most vulnerable.

It was true
that our pink Hamtaro shirts matched.
But that was no reason for such taunting.

We turned our backs to them and continued to talk.
"Hey Fred! I'm talking to you." They knew his name.

We ignored once again.
"How can you wear pink like that? You're a dude."
Someone dressed all in black put in his part,
"Do not insult the color pink or Hamtaro around me!"

The group was stunned.
The line began to move slowly again
and took us far enough away from them
that we didn't hear them anymore.

I looked at him,
concerned.
"I get that all the time,"
he said to me.

I didn't know what
I should say to him.
"They're just jealous,
because they don't get to hang out

with beautiful women."
I smiled,
and the line continued to move.
We were a step ahead of the world.

Anomalies: My Struggle for an Identity

Erika Drain
First Place for High School Prose, 2012 (Tie)

Everyone desires to stand out. No matter the profession they wish to pursue, the effort they put into their reputation, or the reasons that motivate them to do so, succeeding is always the main goal.

When I was young, I loved the idea of being someone unique. A girl who stands out against the crowd and whose work and ideas can count for something in the future. I studied, I researched, I experienced the world as best as I could, and yet, there was a barrier. I never thought about my race as something that defined me.

With every standardized test, I marked the clear bubble "Black/African American" without a second thought. I actually thought of it as impractical; why in the world would they need to know that? It's not like it changes my score, I thought. I had eventually achieved my lifelong goal of individualism and realized it was much harder than I believed. It wasn't until I had begun accomplishing something with my knowledge and skills that I realized how much that bubble on that page actually meant.

I've been labeled and categorized as a variety of titles throughout my life. "Silly," I could agree with; "weird," I could live with; "black," I was forced to accept. However, I don't endure the projected hatred that was so prevalent during Dr. Martin Luther King's time. I have friends of every different shade and every origin. I've gone to two schools: one a public school with the majority of the students being African American, and currently a private school that has more diversity in its student body. The transition was odd, as I've never been a minority—as defined by the color of my skin at least. With my final goodbyes to my elementary school memories, I realized how out of place I've really been. As a straight-A student at the time, I was constantly criticized as "too smart." Being described as a person who is "not black enough" shocked me even more. I can't remember what scared me more: the idea that there was ever a thing as too smart, or the air of inferiority my friends had towards me. In my mind, I was just as "black" as the rest of them. Metaphorically speaking, I was the black sheep in my class. In my entire school. I was singled out among my many friends.

But to many, I was not black.

"What does this mean?" I thought to myself. What does black actually mean, and why doesn't it seem to fit with my identity according to many people I identify with? Since when did my character determine whom I was supposed to represent on the outside? Dr. King once said that he hoped to "look to a day when people will not be judged by the color of their skin, but by the content of their character." What would he say if the same people are, in fact, being judged by their character, but are being compared and discriminated against because it may not "fit" with the stereotypes attached to the color of their skin? Since when is intelligence a personality trait of

Caucasians? When did the diverse genres of music I listen to—I've recently gained an obsession with Korean pop—make me an anomaly in the black community? All of these questions swirled around in my head, and I started to believe what people were actually saying about me: I'm just not black enough.

About two years later, I was a rising sophomore at Winchester Thurston. I pursued the same goal of developing my character, but I still questioned the definition of black. I shied away from most of the students, hoping that they would just make a label for me that I could live with. Despite this, my personality shone through, and I made friends, like any other high school student. However, compared to my old school, there were very few African American students who really accepted me. I was fine with this; I had friends, and that's all that mattered. By then, I was a competitive rower for my school's crew team, I was a major trumpet player in Winchester Thurston's jazz band, and I had pretty decent grades. I was finally happy, and I thought I had found a place where I belonged. I didn't think I was seen as "not black enough."

During that Thanksgiving break, however, I had an encounter that shook my confidence. I was accustomed to answering questions from older people about the reality of attending a private school. "What are the students like?" was in the top ten. I gave bromides as responses, and they usually accepted them. But one day, I was asked about my rowing career:

"What in the hell kind of a sport is crew for a person like you?"

I was puzzled. "I love rowing," I replied.

"Rowing? That's not like you. You're too big anyway, and when's the last time you've seen a black girl in a boat? I guess you aren't that black after all. I knew those white people would change you."

And just like that, my hopes were dashed. Besides my self-esteem about my weight being crushed into the dirt, everything I believed about my greater community became a lie at that point. From the words of an elder, I'm not black. How could I give up something I was so passionate about in order to be accepted? I recognized that no matter what I do, the color of my skin will scream "black" to a person of any other color, and to blacks, I am just a mistake. A failure to uphold the current black stereotypes that everyone knows about. An anomaly.

Two months ago, I watched the documentary *Black Is . . . Black Ain't* by Marlon Riggs, and it inspired me to truly think about who I am as an African American— or, who I thought I was. According to Riggs, because one's black identity was so often limited, distorted and made shameful by whites, asserting a new black identity became important to many African Americans. His camera traverses the country, coming face to face with black people young and old, rich and poor, rural and urban, gay and straight, who are grappling with the paradox of several, often contested, definitions of "blackness"—just like me. Additionally, generalizations are being imposed upon African Americans not only by those outside the race, but by black people themselves. I was surprised that I wasn't the only one enduring this discrimination and relieved as well. Furthermore, every skin color has a set of beliefs portrayed by the media or just word-of-mouth to the public. How could I protest my lack of inclusion in the black community, when those of other races are suffering the same struggle? Maybe anomalies aren't the issue: labels based on appearance are. No one should feel discriminated against because their personality doesn't fit these labels.

The war that Dr. King fought against discrimination is by no means over; the battle of white versus black may have been won, but not the battle of an individual versus his/her corresponding stereotypes, which is a battle that I have been fighting my entire life. A battle for many individuals whose complexion, class, speech, intellect, religion, gender, or sexual orientation has made them feel like anomalies to the stereotypes they have been fighting against. To this day, I realize that these labels aren't leaving anytime soon. But this doesn't require that I, or anyone else, must live with them. I am me, the hard-working woman that I've aspired to become, and no label can take that away.

Goofy Little White Girl

Brianna Dunleavy
Third Place for High School Poetry, 2001

Summer of '92
I was all of six years
and missing my front teeth.
My bangs were chopped and mangled
like I had paid a drunkard to cut them.
Goofy little white girl.
That's what I was.
Goofy little white girl
who lived in East Liberty.
I didn't like white people.
I only saw beauty in shades of brown.

Summer of '92
I spent my first night over at a friend's house.
There were eight of us.
Seven black,
and me.
Goofy little white girl.
They listened to Kris Kross
and made up little dances.
I had yet to acquire a sense of rhythm.
They plaited and beaded each other's hair.
My hair was too short,
and mangled,
and white.
I had white peoples' hair.
Sitting with them, it was inescapable.
I was a goofy little white girl.

Summer of '92
The temperature rose to 90.
The black cement was scorching
under bare feet.
Porches were lined
with small, sweating black children.
Tons of big brown eyes
looking utterly bored.
Tons of small brown faces
looking utterly hot.

Summer of '92
a big black teenager
with a big white grin
and a big silver wrench
was our godsend.
He took the wrench
and, muscles straining in the heat,
opened up the fire hydrant.
Clear water came gushing out
over sweat-stained brows,
big, brown, smiling faces,
and bright, brown eyes.
Waves of clear water,
waves of brown skin,
and me.
Wet, smiling
goofy little white girl.

Summer of '92
I learned a lesson
while sitting on the black cement
in a sea of black faces
surrounded in clear water.
For that second it no longer mattered
that I was a goofy little white girl,
or if I had been black,
or yellow,
or polka-dotted.
Everything was just wet.
Clear.
The way things should be.

I Am Not Wrong: Wrong Is Not My Name

Elsa Eckenrode
Second Place for High School Poetry, 2017

i.
When I cut my hair
my mother asks if I want to be a boy,
as if this new haircut has transformed my entire being,
and imagine this: the day after,
me, hunched over my kitchen table,
hair short and bleach blond,
my body in an XL black shirt, formless,
not angular or curved, she asks,
is this your butch pose?

ii.
How do I tell her I learned a while ago
to hate my body for what others see?
I learned to cover myself up
because when it's 9 p.m. and I'm walking home by myself
I am: all skinny jeans and body outlined,
I'm nothing more to the man outside than
some dyke he'd love to see in bed,
but how do I tell him
I am more than just a body?

iii.
What does it matter
if my mom sees me as a butch
and men see me as a fetish
when at the end of the day I'm still thinking
about the first time a guy called me
a faggot for not flirting with him.
Why couldn't I tell him he was wrong?
I was 14.
Will he ever know how scary
it is to be told you're unnatural?

iv.
And one night three years later, at 17,
my dad's girlfriend sits me down for girl talk
and asks me why I don't like men,
but doesn't she understand

we are so much more than bodies?
Why can't I tell her she's wrong?
It's like I'm 14 again,
numb and speechless, breathless.
Does she know how much
my chest hurts to feel so ungodly?

v.
I try to forget the sinking feeling
but it starts eating me alive
and I tell my mom the next day,
broken down and sobbing in her car,
and my dad promises she isn't homophobic
but how can he tell me I'm wrong
when he wasn't there? Why wasn't he there for me?
How do I tell him how hard it is to feel right
when I've spent years learning I was wrong,
but this isn't who I am, I swear I'm so much more.
I am not wrong. Wrong is not my name.

Shiksa

Carolyn Elliott
Honorable Mention for High School Prose, 2001

He called me Woman, so I called him Boy. We worked on physics problems together, studied Shakespeare, talked about books. He studied Marxism and had the Manifesto on a shelf by his bed. I liked his body: short, broad shouldered, compact and quick. I liked his black hair and his Jewish nose.

Boy's father was a retired rabbi. Julie, my lily-white and Catholic best friend, loved to watch movies like *Fiddler on the Roof* and *Yentil*. She said I wasn't good enough for a rabbi's son. Julie let me know I was a *shiksa*.

One Friday after school, I walked with Boy down a main street of his predominantly Jewish neighborhood, Squirrel Hill. I mentioned Julie's term for me to Boy. He laughed and put his headphones on. As we walked, Boy listened to rap music, to Mos Def and Dr. Octagon. After a time, he passed his headphones to me and let me listen for a few minutes. I passed them back to him.

"The lyrics are too fast; I can't understand the song. How can you?"

"Woman, you're just too slow. I'm used to it."

We walked by some girls in long skirts, long ponytails and tennis shoes: Orthodox girls, straight out of the Yeshiva. Boy looked at them and said to me, "Better a *shiksa* than one of those."

In his room, Boy changed his shirt. Like all of his clothes, the shirts were Triple Five Soul, a hip-hop brand favored by black rappers. We sat, talked, and kissed. I tried to make friends with his cats, whom he loved more than anything or anyone. His cats curled in his lap, on his shoulders, and he cooed tender baby talk to them.

Then I sat down for Sabbath dinner with Boy's family. His father wanted him to wear a yarmulke; Boy refused, so they compromised with Boy wearing a Triple Five Soul hat to cover his head. Boy leaned back from the table. I leaned in. I liked to hear the rabbi singing and blessing; it was more interesting than Grace.

For Hanukkah, I went over Boy's house and brought him a tin of Italian Christmas cookies that my mother made: pizzelles and chocolate-covered biscotti. He told me, "Woman, I would love you, but you're not black and you're not a cat."

"You're not black either, Boy."

"Yes, I am."

"How do you figure?"

"Woman, I just am."

The next week, Boy said we weren't officially a couple. He took a beautiful black girl out on a few dates. She refused to kiss him, though. She told her friends he was trying too hard, then she told him she just wanted to be friends.

A little while later, Boy and I broke up. Julie said she always knew I didn't deserve a rabbi's son. I still see Boy often at school, but he doesn't call me Woman anymore, he calls me by my name. I think he's dating a nice Jewish girl.

I Never Wore an Ethnic Dress

Alayna Frankenberry
Third Place for College Prose, 2007

I never marched in a nationality parade
or drew a family tree, or said these are his
eyes, her mouth, it runs in the family.
I looked for myself in strangers, stood
in a grocery aisle surveying the slope
of a woman's nose, the color of her hair.

I never felt hurt by a racist joke, never visited
a concentration camp or a burial mound
clutching my chest, the old oppressed
blood still beating on. I never got a letter
the way my sister got a letter, never analyzed
the handwriting, questioning the love
in the scribbled *love*.

I only ever whispered *I hate* to my parents
who weren't there to hear me. I only ever
screamed *I love* to my family that is, cried
with my family that is, camped in the backyard,
built birthday cakes in the sand, watched
thunderstorms from the patio, huddled
together with my family that is. And I learned
more each year, what that word means.
But I never wore an ethnic dress.

White Coat

Gretchen Gally
First Place for High School Prose, 2006

Lawn chairs, stools and recliners taken from the garbage rose up from the small patch of dirt situated at the bottom of the auction house. The oldest farmers and best breeders sat in the recliners, their feet up on the wooden plank that kept the bidders from falling into the pit with the auction cattle, sheep, pigs, goats, or occasional mule. The stench of dirt and sweat from the show ring, or the men, was so strong that it stung the inside of my nose. I winced and held up my hand, hoping that the scent of soap and lotion could cover it. My cousin, Jenny, born and raised on a farm, breathed normally.

"City-girl don't like the farm animals," my aunt teased. She patted my shoulder, gingerly, not to get my white coat dirty. I smiled.

"It's not just the animals." I pointed down to one of the Amish people wearing a heavy woolen shirt and black boots with laces. He had bowl cut hair and yellow teeth.

"That's Jonah," Jenny said. "He helped build our barn."

The man looked up from filling his pipe, his hands working swiftly over the tobacco and packing it into the bowl. They were brown hands, stained from hard work and hours out in the fields guiding horses and plows. He looked up and around the auction house when his eyes met mine. He smiled, but I turned my back on him.

"How long do these things usually last?" I asked.

"Usually an hour or two, depending on how hot the bidding gets, or how much stock was brought." Jenny looked over my shoulder. "Jonah's coming over. Be polite."

"Polite? What?"

The man called Jonah showed up at my elbow. He held his pipe in his left hand, using the other to tip his hat to my aunt, cousin, and finally me.

"Ladies, how are you?" When he spoke, I expected broken English to come out. Instead, his German accent rolled out with the words and filled the space between us with something of tradition and lost culture, something different from myself. "Are you planning on buying any animals, young lady?"

"Me?"

"Her?" My cousin laughed and leaned against the back of a chair to support herself.

"Jonah, this is my niece, Sarah. She's visiting from Pittsburgh." My aunt put her arm around my shoulder.

"All the way from Pittsburgh? It's nice to meet you, Sarah." Jonah wiped his hand on his gray homemade pants before he held it out to me to shake. I stared at it. "I'm Jonah Yoder."

I paused too long and I felt a finger in the small of back from my aunt. I looked up to her; she scowled. I carefully stuck my hand out of my pocket and gave Jonah's hand a quick rattle. His hand was rough against mine, like he worked too hard or I didn't work hard enough.

"How long are you staying, Sarah?"

"Five days," I mumbled.

"You should be careful not to ruin that white coat while you're up here," he said. "Lots of dirt floating around."

"I'll be careful, thanks." I lifted the hand he shook up to my nose.

Trying to be casual, I smelled it.

"Okay. Well, Pat, it was nice to see you again." Jonah nodded to my aunt and headed back to the cluster of other Amish people on the other side of the level. I let out the audible breath I didn't know I was holding.

"I don't like to mingle with them, either," the old man sitting in the chair Jenny was leaning on said. He turned himself around and took off his trucker hat and put it in the pocket of his oversized flannel coat. "They're just dirty to me."

Aunt Pat opened her mouth to speak, but stopped. Jenny stared at me, flicking a piece of her blond hair out of her eyes.

"I especially wouldn't want to touch them wearing white either. Never seen an Amish that didn't ruin everything they touched."

"Ruin?"

"When my father was building our fence line—I live on Rycole Road—he had some Amish from down the road help with the lumber. Those men wasted more wire and wood than my father could afford! Had to sell off some of the horses because they wouldn't stay in without a good fence."

"I'm sure it wasn't just the Amish's fault," my aunt said.

"You'd be surprised at what them Amish can do. Can't trust a single one of them. Always wanting rides in the car, borrow a telephone."

"Sarah," Jenny cocked her head back to the side, "let's go."

I stumbled over my Aunt Pat's foot as we headed down the dusty hallway to the balcony overlooking the incoming animals. She walked quickly, so I had to skip to keep up with her. She stopped short as she came to the walkway and walked carefully, slowly, over the animals.

"I didn't want to hear anymore of that bull." Jenny rested her hands on the wooden railing. The cows below us shuffled in the dirt and mooed loudly.

"Yeah," I said, only half-heartedly. I didn't see what that man was so wrong about. Even my aunt had said that they didn't do the best job on her barn. I didn't like the Amish, either.

"I don't know where those old guys get off putting other people down like that. Just because they are a little different. At least they aren't screwing around with other peoples' wives like *that* guy." She unzipped her outer jacket. "They might have different beliefs than us, but you know what I mean. They're still people."

"I guess so." They were too different, though. People or not, they were like a whole other species, native to Germany, but raised in captivity around the Pennsylvania area.

"Animals," I mumbled.

I kicked a pebble into the crack between the wood planks. It hit a pig and it squealed. I looked over the railing to the mass of bodies moving below me like a churning sea. All the pigs were trapped in a wooden crate, pushing their snouts into each other's bodies, eating each other's tails. They squealed like the last scene in a horror film, like animals. I thought of Jonah, calling him an animal, thinking that he wore clothes and he spoke English and he made art. Pigs didn't do that; they ate their own tails. They were the animals. They were.

"Sarah, don't do that." Jenny tapped the top of my shoe. I looked up, startled.

"Nobody wants to hear them cry. You know, I heard that pig skin is just as sensitive as a human's."

I looked up at her, my hands in my pockets. "I'm sorry," I said. "I won't do it again."

"Oh, I don't care, I just don't want us to get yelled at." She flashed a smile that I recognized in her mother. "Let's go back to the auction. My mom might buy something this time."

She started to shuffle along the walkway. I pulled my hands out of my pocket and touched the railing.

"Jenny, is it true that their skin is as sensitive as a human's?"

"No." She turned around and laughed. "But I thought it sounded nice."

Wife

Hannah Geisler
First Place for High School Poetry, 2016

(after Jamaica Kincaid)

wear
      red/
            dresses
and yellow latex gloves.
      choke   /yourself
with a noose of delicately brilliant
pearls   and finger the scars
like a chocolate/ diamond necklace.
          never wear ripped stockings
never wear fringe or lace
      you slut
be humble
      and meek
          seen/not/heard
and when you do speak, share   gossip/beef stew recipes
          tell me/ about grandma's county/ fair cobbler
      does molasses /   stain cotton?

curl your hair every day
and then tie it away from your face
never let him see/   you sweat.
      get excited over aprons/ watch infomercials
and then call your   girlfriends
      to brag about your latest gadgets.

          never stop/   working
never set down the sponge
      lotion your hands
twice a day to help with the   bleeding
      get down on your knees/ polish the china/ dinner at 5 o'clock.
buy lingerie
      sexy
         black
           lingerie
and surprise   him after work   wear it
      that night/ and every night after that / and any other time

                 that he tells you.

Questions for a Black Mother

Suhail Gharaibeh-Gonzalez
Second Place for High School Poetry, 2016

for Aiyana Mo'Nay Stanley-Jones

mommy mommy what's a police state?

A SWAT team launches a flash-bang grenade through a window.
It shatters out a song
and the orchestra of cop-blue night feeds in through the broken glass.

See, we're in the colored section, twenty-ten—
boarded-up windows.
Graffiti pops on the side of abandoned buildings.
No playgrounds here—
weeds grow tall instead.

mommy mommy what's apartheid?

The grenade has burnt up the edge of a Disney Princess blanket.
They kick down the door
and plunge into the house.

An officer's gun cocks back. *bang.*

A bullet slices through the air, and it makes home
in a seven-year-old's head. She's asleep on the couch,
next to her grandmother. It obliterates fresh knowledge—
how to spell "cat" and how two plus two equals four.
The SWAT team kicked down the door
and the little black girl was sleeping,
she was playing dead anyway,
she wasn't alive anyway,
she wasn't human anyway anyway anyway—
black bodies plastered on tv screens.
Cracked backs, gunshots,
turning clocks, and every minute the pool of blood soaks deeper,
autopsies, genocide by proxy,
and these very urban soldiers
appear smiling on the eleven o'clock news.
Their badges shine.

mommy mommy what's desensitization?

Fluorescent lights spin.
Red carnations bloom on the little girl's pillow.
Her grandmother holds her and weeps.
January twenty-fifteen. The officer who fired the gun is acquitted of all charges.
Tears flood all of Detroit.

The news spews distortion:
Aiyana's grandmother reached for the gun!

Did you mistake her hand flying out to stop the bullet?
Maybe she was reaching for survival,
for humanity,
for protection.

The news spews the logistics of these ballistics,
offering explanations for murder, but it's simple:
since slave ships first docked here,
the wombs of black women have been
graveyards for their future children,
fate sealed by the effigy of his race
because black children are always black before innocent—
but officer Joseph Weekley's mother smiled and beamed
when he joined the police academy, saying
"he has so much
promise."

Hip-Hop Workshop, November 28, 2002

Gillian Goldberg
Second Place for High School Poetry, 2003

The girls at the back don't even bother to whisper. *How's two white boys gonna teach us about hip-hop?* And something in it reminds me of the limp in Kelsey's face when they tell her black boys don't play hockey, and they make their eyes wide when she tells them her brother is a forward and he scored three goals yesterday but her face is still limp. Or maybe it's the scars on her brother's face that he covered with cocoa butter for a year. I never knew you could use cocoa butter to cure cuts, but I knew people got beat up for walking late in parks. Mostly, it reminds me of the music Kelsey gave me, sitting at my feet in my coat pocket, and my coat is warm in winter, and the music is burning a hole, pounding, like a heart, like a fist, giving me away.

Canto Immigrante

Kevin González
Third Prize for College Poetry, 2002

I did not come to your country for dreams—
I am still here

though I never encountered a spirit
to sink in a river

or a rain that could fit in my pocket.
I tripped on your culture

but did not fall. You came bearing
a barbed carpet.

I countered with the edge of a tired glance.
I know order exists

somewhere between the freight of our fists.
I too have pleaded clouds

and stood under streetlamps smoking
strayed nights—my smoke

blending pacific. My shadow will never apologize
from under your feet.

Shelter

Kevin González
Second Place for College Poetry, 2003

The Prime Minister of Israel is Downtown. A friend calls—
he will be on the news, carrying a coffin

draped in a Palestinian flag. He wants to come over,
let the mottled glow of my television coat him.

It's 10:30pm on a Tuesday in Pittsburgh. I have not been
to a march since I left Puerto Rico. I have stopped

watching the news since Bush was *elected*?
"I'm about to go to my P.O. box," I say

as I slide my feet into shoes, fumble my keys,
briefly hoping for a letter from home. I don't say

I'd rather freeze for 20 minutes in the broken rectangle
of a bus shelter than watch him lug around a coffin.

I don't say I'm *tired* or *bleak* or *I've lost faith in human
compassion.* The black bus driver only greets black passengers—

I sit right behind him, stain of sun faded on my skin.
I wish I could crawl into my P.O. box

and sleep through the cold, tucked between
the soft glossy pages of a catalog. That's all I got

today. I should have said, "It's okay, man,
you can say *you're welcome,* cause

I've been through shit too." On the return bus,
a girl's neck cradles her cell phone, "But baby, you

just broke up with me. Baby, you're hurting my ear.
Baby, you just can't hit me like that, you just can't."

We've all been through shit, too. Walking up my street,
I wave the rolled up catalog as if I were directing

an orchestra of wind. On the other sidewalk,
a white man walking and a black man on a bicycle

are coming toward each other.
The black man screams but the white man does not move.

"Move, move you asshole." But he does not move.
I stop and grip the catalog, my palm polishing it

with sweat. The white man kicks the front wheel
as the bike tries to dodge him. I flinch at the scrape of a face

on asphalt, a forehead drawing its oblong print of blood.
I am tired. I am bleak. I have lost faith in human compassion.

They have started bombing Vieques again. They have not freed
Mumia Abu Jamal. He hit her. Caskets draped in flags.

"Who's the asshole now?" the white man sprints off,
the drumming of his sneakers a symphony of suspense.

The black man lifts his bike and pedals after him.
As they round the corner onto the Avenue, I think of home,

the place I started. I am so far away, a block
from my apartment in this cold and foreign city. My hand

is the only part that fits in the shelter of my P. O. box.
"I love you too, baby," she said, "forgive me for crying."

Proud to Be

Emily Green
First Place for College Poetry, 2003

In grade school / they showed us a film strip
Proud to Be Me / each strange hair / oddly shaped
nose / even webbed feet / proud to be
and that's what I mean / with this white
thing / with the not-regretting-my-skin-so-pale-
it-gleams-translucent-thing
and not sorry / my eyes
so blue / my hair spit with blond

shame hails from / another place
the decision to stand / on the last-run
late-night bus / instead / of sit
by / the old man / maybe he's black
and should i forgive / my fear / maybe
he's white / and ragged / homeless
too close / to a class / i might have / taken

who do you love / the song / asks
who do you love / i ask you / who do you
hate / the white / white face
of a ghoul like me / what i'm proud
to be / is not / what i've heard myself
say / don't say homophobic things
i have gay friends / and know it's bad
to label friends / bad to single out
just as / bad / not to / come out
with the truth / of desiring both / sexes

projector / with tape recorder / ding-
ed when the image / changed / teacher
never chose me / to turn it / prejudice
isn't that / easy / even if I told you
she knew / my family is catholic
if you knew / my father worked
at McDonald's / my mother
was three months / in / when she
married / not that easy

i am proud / and transparent / i am catholic
and bisexual / i am sorry / for every imperfection
that keeps me / two steps / from you / if the filmstrip
had a soundtrack / i'd sing / to you / if someone
set me / afire / i'd sing louder / how long
could you stay / still / how long can we / not listen /

Chocolate and Vanilla

Mya Green
Second Place for High School Poetry, 2002

TaMisha and I went
to the Sarah Heinz House
building every Tuesday after school.
And every day, we walked into the building hand in hand,
terrified of the white girls
that roamed on every floor.
I was eight years old,
and TaMisha was twelve.
Tuesday was swimming day,
so we had to get dressed.
Walking back into the locker rooms,
clinging to TaMisha's left arm,
we staggered through a soul train line
of dirty looks and smirks.
Crammed into one bathroom stall,
we struggled to put our bathing suits on.
We didn't want them to see our skin
or our scars.
Momma once told me that chocolate
and vanilla didn't mix.
We listened for the locker room to clear
of loud chuckles, screams, and wet feet
slapping against the tiles.
Shoulder to shoulder in the tiny stall,
wrapped in our small blue towels,
we tiptoed out of the locker room,
and slid into the showers.
The steaming water burned
my chocolate body.
I wanted to know what it felt like
to be popular.
I wanted to have straight, sassy
hair and smooth legs.
Instead, I had hair that I now
saw as nappy and legs that were
scrawny and useless.
As we stepped out of the showers
onto the cold, damp floor, the steam
followed us to the pool.

Jill, the gym teacher, rolled her eyes
at us.
I could see the veins bulging
out of her neck.
She swallowed hard and told us
to get in.
The water rippled rapidly away from us
as we put our toes into the water.
We stayed on the shallow side of the rope.
TaMisha and I couldn't swim
and we would never learn.
I watched the girls punch the volleyball
back and forth over the net.
TaMisha was floating alone in the corner,
practicing how to hold her breath.
I was wishing I could replace
TaMisha with one of those deep-end
girls and hold them under the water,
just long enough so that they reached
the surface gasping for forgiveness.
I floated closer to the rope
so I could watch them play the game,
and I saw them whispering.
I'm sure I heard them say
that I was polluting the water.
A few seconds later, the ball flew
over the rope and hit me in the face.
It hit with a force that sent
blood showering into the pool.
The girls jumped out of the water
sending shrill screams and laughter
bouncing off the walls.
With my busted nose, I cried,
climbing out of the pool.
My tears and blood mixed
together and found their way
to the crease of my lips.
tasting like injustice.
I looked back into the pool,

and like vinegar and oil,
my blood separated in the water.
Jill moved slowly toward me
and told me to go to the nurse.
TaMisha and I walked down the hall
in our wet bathing suits.
Shivering and feeling half naked,
we walked on the cold marble floor,
searching for the door that said "Nurse."
When we reached the office,
there was another girl there,
stretched out on the resting bench,
holding an icepack on her pale, blue ankle.
The nurse gave me a plastic bag
with three ice cubes in it,
instead of a pack,
and made me sit in a rusted,
brown chair with particles of paint
falling from it.
I was sent home twenty minutes later,
holding that baggy of warm water
up to my face.
My nose was red, scratched, and swollen.
Little drops of warm blood trickled
down and stained the little hairs
above my lip.
Every time I scrunched my face
or had the motive to sneeze, my nose
shriveled up and made my eyes water.
TaMisha kept telling me it was going to be okay.
And at that moment, I knew that it wasn't.
"Okay" was her way of saying that it wouldn't
happen again.
Or that it would, just not to me.
Ever since I was a child,
My momma told me to be proud
that I was black.
Walking out of the building, I knew
I had let her down.

My pride had been shattered into pieces
by a single game of volleyball.
When we got home, I told my momma everything.
She took us out for ice cream
to try to cheer us up.
"Thank you for being strong,"
she said, looking at me
in the rearview mirror.
I forced a smile on my face
which sent a sharp pain through my cheeks.
My nose still felt broken.
When we arrived, the lady asked
us what flavor we wanted.
When TaMisha chose chocolate and vanilla
swirl, I looked at her.
I chose strawberry.

Some Hip-Hop Show

Nicholas Hall
First Place for High School Prose, 2001

Music is shaking this bright midsummer day. Bumping vibrant air into our bodies, pushing us into thick oscillations to broken beats. The papery cotton of my white Oxford shirt rubs against the thick softness of hoodies at my left and right.

I think about my mom's usual reaction to this music: not a favorable one at all. She wants melody and can't justify the lyrics' meaning for the beauty of their beat. I think about her metered didactics on community and the trends of isolation and distrust rising in our society, on how they move her.

Then the music pipes off. Some fuse has broken. The circuitry of this park cannot handle the power it takes to bring unity to this peppered crowd. All bodies land in some pose for a second, having just been reborn into a rhythmless world. They start to scan their surroundings. Some hip-hop elder feels the judgments bubble up a little, the heavy throb that had been hammering it down now gone.

"Beat box!" he yells. "Beat box!"

An MC to the left picks up where the dead turntables left off. He starts spitting and hissing. He is alone for a second but knows we need time to come back. An MC to the right pops his hands together over his head and scans us like a wise father. The MC to the center charges up his lungs and calls us to clapping, "'Cause they ain't no music 'less we makin' it."

Hands come together. Then they come together harder. The MCs left, right and center are respectively spitting, clapping, and calling for us to clap harder, to bring back the thump. We try with all we have to tell ourselves, to tell each other, that the circuitry of our humanity can handle the power it takes to bring unity to this crowd.

The music booms back on and we cheer and try to believe that we need it.

My First Best Friend

Arica L. Hayes
Third Place for High School Poetry, 2004

I was born with multiple ethnic backgrounds,
but by looking at me one couldn't tell;
I simply looked like a light-skinned African American child.
That's what I thought I was anyway.

My first best friend, well, she was the opposite.
She was Russian and Italian.
Her skin was as pale as snow,
she almost looked like Snow White.
She was an adorable kid.

When we were young,
we were inseparable like Siamese twins.
Our differences didn't matter to us.
We were just two adventurous little girls.

We were so close that we even bathed together.
Every night we would take turns staying at each other's houses.
If we hadn't looked so different, you would swear we were sisters.
I even called her mother "Mom," and she did the same with mine.

When we got a little bit older, we would sneak out of the house
at night just to play games with other children.
Sometimes our adventures would lead us to the dark dreary woods,
where my friend and I got stuck in a patch of thorns. We were scared.

The Spice Girls came out, and we had so much fun
pretending to be them. She was Ginger and I was Scary.
We had on so much glitter and make-up that we looked like two disco balls
walking around in Spice Girl shoes.

Then we got older and started making new friends.
Our friendship died as flowers do, when summer is over.
I guess our summer had ended. We grew apart
and straight into the world of racism.

My new friends told me that she didn't matter,
and that she was just some white girl who thinks she's better than me.
When our friendship came to its demise, so did my individuality
because I believed them. It was far from summer now; winter was here.

My ex-friend must have been the brains of our long-ago schemes
because as racist as I had become, I didn't notice half my family looked white.
I loved them more than anything even though they were white,
just like the friend I discarded like a bad memory.

One day at my family reunion, I was looking through a photo album.
I always loved to see people in my family. Then I saw an old picture
of a young white woman. My eyes grew wide as I tried to conjure the reason.
I went back and forth through possibilities like the ocean tides go back and forth.

Finally, after minutes of brain-racking thinking, I asked.
My cousin Desiree told me that the woman was Grandma Hayes.
She, the white lady, was my grandma.
I took a closer look at her as she stared at me.
Yes, she was white. Yes, my facial features favored hers.

All my thoughts seemed to come crashing down, like the crashing ocean waves.
My whole way of thinking had been ruined by a picture.
True, my parents had never taught me to be a racist,
but it was my friends' opinions that mattered.

For some odd reason I remembered my sixth-grade ski trip.
Some boy spat on me, and it was my friend
who took time out of her trip to find him and do what any good friend would.
Finally I realized that it was my fault the friendship ended.

I wanted to apologize to her badly. The need was like the need
to scratch an annoying itch. I didn't know if she would accept.
I was tired of not doing what I wanted to do.
All those years ago I wanted to tell my new enemies to shut up.

When I saw her, I was ready to apologize.
I took a few deep breaths, and the air felt like it was choking me;
I was so nervous. Then without any warning, my feet worked by themselves.
I started walking toward her, hesitantly. Then she threw her arms around me.

I'll never be sure if she felt the tear drop on her neck,
snaking a path down her back when she called me my old nickname.
She said, "Ri, you're so big! I've missed you."
I hugged her tighter feeling warmth and said, "I've missed you too, Alyssa."

Halloween in the Welfare Office

Desiree Henry
First Place for High School Poetry, 2002

On the sidewalk outside
eyes search my body.
I can feel them running up and down
the vertical of my legs and the horizontal
of my face.
I look left and right, seeing if anyone
points or shakes their head.

I step into a small square room,
an old onion smell lies stagnant on the air.
There are dozens of people,
children are spread out on the floor
playing with the dust bunnies under
their mothers' chairs.
One takes hold of my attention,
she resembles my daughter.
She wears a torn black T-shirt with red
stretch pants, a black rose up the leg.
Beautiful little girl, long black hair, blue eyes,
pale as the ghost hanging from the ceiling.
She looks up when I walk past; as we make
eye contact, I wave.
She does not respond.

There is a thick, redheaded, white woman
behind the counter, talking on the phone.
She looks at me as if I am a fly as she goes to retrieve a newspaper.
Oh my. Yes girl, I know exactly what you mean!
Uh huh . . . I knock on the glass
that separates us.
I'm here to pick up my check.
She tells me that I must wait
and that someone will assist me when available.
She rolls her eyes in her head, turns her back
and resumes her conversation.

I sit in one of the sunken-in, brown, polyester chairs.
The springs protrude out the side, and the arms
are almost completely torn off.
I look around the tiny space filled with lively

bodies, and my eyes stray back
to the little girl.
She intrigues me.

The girl's mother whispers something
into her ear, still no response.
I put my nose in the air;
someone has on White Diamonds, my favorite perfume.
It is the old white woman on my right, she wears
a bright red jumpsuit with black trimming.
Her sunglasses are as black as the skeleton's
eye sockets on the poster warning not to drink
and drive at the counter up front.
I smile and continue to wait.
Smith, they call as I move to the next seat;
the old woman gets up slowly and walks
to the gray-haired man who beckons to her.
I am now by the little girl.

I ask her, what is wrong, why so down?
She looks at her mother and then at me,
lifts a pale hand and puts it on top of mine.
Her touch is cold as the vanilla ice cream
she spilled on her pants. Small fingertips
on the back of my hand,
a sensation of brushing against my satin.

Just as quick
the girl's mother grabs her
and takes her into the restroom.
They return what seems like years later,
and sit on the other side of the room.
The girl's hands are a bright red,
you can see the layer of skin
that has peeled away, raw
and with no protection.

A smell of pink soap fresh out
of the dispenser—so strong that my eyes
begin to water.

I move closer to the counter, trying
to escape the aroma of lilacs and roses.

Why did they stay in the bathroom for so long?
It was no business of mine, but in her absence
I felt dismal, like a child feels when she loses
a precious toy.
She was about to say something to me
when her mother took her away.
Right then it hit me . . .
I knew why her hands were red.
I knew why the sidewalk strangers
looked at me.
The blond-haired woman took the angel
and washed her cloud-colored hands,
washed them until they bled, until she
remembered why she isn't supposed to talk
to anyone who walks through that door.

That I wasn't one of the exceptions,
her mother whispered in her ear.

Dusty Memories

Lauren Hirata
Second Place for College Prose, 2012

A dry desert wind whips at the low-lying brush at our feet. There isn't shade for miles, and sweat is starting to bead on my nose. In the distance, the Sierra Nevadas taunt us with their snow preserved by high altitude.

We are only two-thirds through our journey to June Mountain—230 miles away from our home in Los Angeles—for our annual fishing trip. Usually, my father drives the 345-mile journey to June Mountain in one straight shot—other than two allotted bathroom breaks—but this time he wanted to make an extra stop at Manzanar National Historic Site. Every other time we've driven past, a simple, "There's Manzanar. That's where Grandma was," sufficed.

Manzanar War Relocation Center was one of ten camps where Japanese Americans were interned during World War II. My grandmother was interned at Manzanar for two years before she asked for permission to leave and move to Milwaukee, Wisconsin, where she stayed until the end of the war.

This particular trip to June Mountain was different from the start. My grandmother was riding with us—she usually drove up separately—and my father decided that this new passenger would be a good segue into a field trip—especially since it's 2002, sixty years since my grandmother was at Manzanar.

Up until this point, my grandmother rarely talked about her experience, and no one in the family wanted to pry. My grandmother hadn't been back since she left in 1944. Since then, the Manzanar National Historic Site was established to preserve the stories of World War II internees, "and to serve as a reminder to this and future generations of the fragility of American civil liberties."

"We lived somewhere around here," says my grandmother, who fidgets with her beaded bracelet and shuffles ahead of the rest of the family. Everybody surveys the desolate landscape around us; small signposts mark distances of 50 yards down the dusty clearing, depicting where wooden barracks would have been. We hurry after my grandmother before the dust can swallow her petite frame.

President Roosevelt's Executive Order 9066 in 1942 called for the relocation of over 110,000 Japanese Americans who lived along the Pacific Coast, and at the time, my grandmother Tomoe (Carole) Kuse was seventeen years old. She had just recently finished high school and was living and working as a housekeeper and nanny in Sacramento, California, trying to save enough money to put herself through beauty school.

However, with the internment authorization, she was given a ten-day warning and had to return to the rest of her family, who lived in a small town outside the city called Elk Grove. My grandmother, her parents, and her four siblings were not given the full ten days to prepare, and instead were evacuated to Manzanar War Relocation Camp within three days.

"We were told to pack up our stuff and get ready to go," my grandmother says.

"So in three days, my mother—you know, Bachan—packed up everything and everyone had a suitcase full of our clothes and whatever else we mainly needed. We boarded the train and headed to Manzanar."

My grandmother sits quietly on a footstool in her kitchen, surrounded by the mix of awkward school portraits of unfortunate haircuts and braces, homemade birthday cards, and family pictures that litter the typical American grandparent's house.

Over 10,000 people made similar trips to Manzanar and, like my grandmother's family, had to sell off their entire lives—furniture, houses, and businesses—as well as leave their friends behind. Some families were split up, including my grandmother's. Her recently married sister and husband were not sent to Manzanar and didn't see the rest of the family until after World War II was over. Despite these unfortunate circumstances and having to put her college aspirations on hold, my grandmother explains that it wasn't she who suffered.

"It was the Issei who lost everything when we were put in camp," she says. "I had just finished school, so it didn't matter too much for me. But it was the older people who really suffered. They lost everything twice: once to emigrate from Japan to America, and again when the war started."

Growing up, my father never asked about my grandmother's experiences at Manzanar. It was always a touchy subject that was just ignored. But when asked now, my grandmother speaks more openly about her experiences at Manzanar. My father thinks it's because her parents—the Issei generation that suffered the most—are long gone.

"In a sense, she's now able to bury the pain away," he says. "She's less haunted by her parents' struggles and hardships now."

She has distanced herself from the past with decades of silence, and can now joke about her experience.

"When we got to camp, I had never seen so many Japanese [people]," she laughs. "I was really surprised—I guess I never realized how many of us were in America. But the thing was, we were all there for the same reason, and that brought us all together."

As a Yonsei, the Japanese term for the Issei's great-grandchildren, I often feel similar to how my grandmother felt as a teenager—that I am often surprised to meet another Japanese American. Unlike my grandmother, though, I feel distanced from the hardships that my relatives had to endure during and after World War II and racial discrimination—at least at this level—is a thing of the past. My friends are color-blind to my ethnicity, as am I sometimes. I consider myself more American than Japanese, and my friends are often taken aback with my skilled use of chopsticks. The one thing that reminds me of my Japanese background is my grandmother and her stories.

"That's not to say that we didn't have problems [in camp] though. I remember there were the people called 'Kibei,' people that were born here but their folks sent them to Japan to study, and then they came back and were put in camp. They were about my age and they started a riot. I wanted to go down there to see what was going on, but my father wouldn't let me—he said it was too dangerous."

Though my grandmother was never interested in learning the details of this event, it turns that this riot was the most serious incident at Manzanar. It occurred at the beginning of December in 1942 and is known as the Manzanar Riot. It raised tensions between prisoners and military guards, and two people were killed.

My grandmother, with her silvery hair in perfect, short pin curls, sits in silence, lost in thought for a brief moment. I watch her think, and my eyes wander to the assortment of crayon-colored papers that are taped to the pantry, and although her kitchen looks like a typical grandmother's, I start to see the Japanese culture seeping into the mix: a ceramic Maneki Neko, or lucky cat, sits perched on a shelf between other knick-knacks; origami koi fish hang from the ceiling; a painting with indecipherable Japanese characters hangs above the sink.

My whole life, I have taken these Japanese symbols for granted and they have blended in with the rest of my environment. Similar to how my family would drive past Manzanar without a second thought, I often found myself celebrating New Year's with Japanese traditions, like eating kuromame—black soybeans—and ozoni—rice cake soup—for good luck, without asking the story behind each tradition.

As we stand in front of a post that says "Block 31," I look around for the block that this sign represents, but there's nothing. The only reminders that this empty clearing used to house over 10,000 people are piles of large white rocks that mark where the doors of the barracks would have been.

"Mom, you lived here?" my father asks, joining me in a search for anything other than brush and dirt. Although he has toured Manzanar once before, he has never been back with his mother.

My grandmother nods, lost in thought. "Two long years," she answers.

Label

Thomas Holmes
Runner-up for High School Nonfiction, 2011

I spent a good part of my life living under a label. In kindergarten I was diagnosed with dysgraphia, a fine motor issue, as well as bilateral coordination issues, which for a kindergartener basically means that I couldn't cut, paste, or color in the lines. Aside from that, a more long-term, non-Crayola-based effect is that I will always have trouble writing. A computer is my equalizer; it is all I really need. Due to my disability, I spent most of my elementary school years in the special education room—I couldn't color in the lines and had terrible handwriting. When I say most of my time, I mean *almost all of it*—not just any time there was writing or spelling or something involving the use of pencil and paper, but also for math, science, social studies, gym, and for a brief period of time in first and second grade, lunch, and the latter two bugged me particularly. Sure, I'll be the first to admit I'm a klutz and I'm not the greatest athlete. However, I've always played sports; I learned to skate at three, but the school's policy about students with mild but identifiable issues was, "Your kind can't do that. We'll have a special activity for you guys." For lunch I was told, "Kids like you are very special and have to have a very special lunch period so we can help you." At the time I wondered how they thought I was alive since apparently I didn't even know how to eat.

The phrases and terms used by teachers and aides to help them describe anyone who was different ("Your kind," "special kids like you," "your group," and my personal favorite, "your friends") gnawed at me. These all came across as strange because I never felt I was a part of any group, as they called the other kids in the resource room. But there wasn't another me. There wasn't even another kid with the same diagnosis as me. "My kind" consisted of the boy who couldn't talk, that girl in the wheelchair, the hyper kid who couldn't sit still and shouted every couple of minutes, and the kid who always looked asleep, whom I was told was slow. These were supposed to be my breed. The term "my friends" never made sense to me, as I had barely spoken to any of them. I had a group of friends who liked me for who I was, though I wasn't supposed to hang out with them because I had "my own group of 'friends' that was just like me," an aide half sneered at me once.

I was viewed as something stupid. To my classmates and teachers, I was something different—not the "different" as in those kids who also got pulled out of class because they were the smart ones who were allowed to read those *Cam Jansen* novels in first grade, while I was struggling to keep a false sense of interest in books with titles like *See Spot Run* after having them read to me for the hundredth time. There was a rule at the school's library that only certain students could get certain books. The smart ones, those who were "gifted," could get those precious novels with only one or two pictures in them. "My kind" received the gifts of picture books that had been so beautifully illustrated with the finest nondescript pictures in which all the characters looked like the victims of a Soviet-era experiment and in the most colorful language stated such words of wisdom as, "The dog is fun."

I kept asking the librarians and my teachers for other books. At one point I grabbed a *Harry Potter* book I was reading at home. The reaction from my teachers was straight out of the manual for SWAT negotiators. It was as if I had taken hostages, was armed, and demanded a helicopter to transport me to a small island country in exchange for their release. In those "everyone's-happy-everyone's-calm" voices I was told, "Drop the book that's out of your range, you can't read that yet, that's not for kids like you, let us help you pick out a nice book you can read."

During this elementary school experience, I was lucky in a lot of ways. I had the support of my parents and a fantastic special education teacher who believed in me as an individual. It is nearly impossible for one to suffer through the truly Sisyphean task of solitarily arguing for a sense of equality. Any activist will almost instantly reach for that hackneyed cliché of "strength in numbers," and it's true. I had people on my side, and that saved me. It gave me the strength to persevere. They worked as advocates on my behalf and, more importantly, showed me my own worth.

We as humans fear the unknown; we also do not want to appear foolish. What ensues is a never-ending sense of fear based on the fact that we tend not to ask simple questions. I do not think that the teachers, aides, and other kids, deep down, were all vicious, hating people, waiting with bated breath to strike at the sound of a wheelchair creaking in the halls or a short bus coming to a stop. I think that the case was simply that they did not know any better.

The best example in my experience was my principal at the time, with whom I did not get on all too well. One time in a meeting with my parents about assisted technology (a computer), he made reference to my "autism." Aside from sending my mother through the roof (which happened quite a bit), this event really did signify something. Here was a man who was an example for the entire school; more than that, he ran it, and he did not have the correct disability down (not even close). He had the access to information, experts, and me, but he chose to ignore it all, and that culture trickled down. You can't blame somebody who truly doesn't know and is only looking up to his or her moral authority figures, but someone who chooses to be ignorant, you can. To quote Dr. King, "Nothing in the world is more dangerous than sincere ignorance and conscientious stupidity."

Flash-forward to seventh grade: I finally was accepted into my school's gifted program with the very same kids who got to read the good books in elementary school. What followed was comical in a melancholy way. Many of the kids I knew, the same kids who hadn't given me a break about being the dumb one or the "retard" in the class, started coming up to me asking, "Holmes, you're smart?" Not in a mocking way, but in that so-surprised voice someone gets when they discover something shocking, but in a good way—apparently about me. The teachers did the same. Both groups started to warm to the idea of me as an equal.

Once I was in their comfort zone of "normalcy," I was able to explain my disability to teachers and students, something I had been trying to do for the previous eight years of my life to no avail. I finally was able to tell people the clear facts. Of course, I said this information in the wonderfully terse and crude speak of a seventh grader, casually explaining, "My handwriting sucks, so I use a computer," but the message was still clear and it was understood.

I was different. I am different. Everyone is. However, I'm still human. Humanity is the single most important thing anyone can have, and yet it is the easiest to lose. Rights and laws are all good and fine. In fact they're wonderful. But humanity, the ability to be viewed as an equal, is something more valuable. When I was labeled, I was some strange, lesser being. What I said didn't matter because I wasn't the same: I was *something less*. This changed in seventh grade when I became an equal to those kids and teachers (well, maybe not completely equal). It meant I was human like them. This struggle for equality, understanding, and the ability to speak openly about my disability is my struggle. Like Dr. King before me, I was taken for something unequal and different, regardless of my own merit.

Writing this essay was a challenge. Writing something my peers would read, and ultimately in some way judge, gave me a slight sense of fear, a sinking feeling that by writing this essay about my disability, once again I would be judged and taken as something other than myself. I would be labeled again. However, I feel that it is in my best interest to write about my disability and, to quote John Milton, "Sally forth and face the adversary." That is, face the stigma attached to disabilities. Dr. King did this. He spoke directly about the issues that faced African Americans and he showed his adversaries and opponents that they were not adversaries, that they were not opponents, but one in the same: people.

Black and White Playground

Dana Horton
First Place for High School Poetry, 2007

The exterior of Alexis's car is leopard print
and matches her pants. Her hair is as pink
as a baby's tongue and hits her face whenever
she tries to dance to the music. She buckles
her seatbelt and changes the song to "Golddigger"
by Kanye West. Her skin is the color of wet wood
and matches her Chanel sunglasses. Alexis starts
to drive. She smiles and pulls a picture out of the
glove department. "That's him. That's my boo.
Brandon. 19. Goes to CCAC. His dad's a lawyer and
his mom's a pharmacist. We met at Club Zoo a
few months ago." Brandon has hair the color copper and
sea-green eyes. I look from the picture to my cousin
and shake my head. I never could picture Alexis
dating a white boy. "Where does he live?" "Upper St.
Clair." The street signs change from blue to green
and we're in the suburbs of Pittsburgh now. The grass
is greener and the houses are bigger. Some houses
take up half the block. Alexis has been driving alone
for the last few months, every single Saturday. I know
where she's going now and I wonder why she always
has to go visit him and why he never comes out to
Homewood and visit her. "Be nice, okay?" Alexis giggles
as she turns the radio on. "Don't do anything to embarrass
me. And don't say anything bad about where we're
going. I promise this won't be long." "We're going to his
house?" Alexis shakes her head and turns the music
down. "Nope." "Then where—" "Stop asking questions.
You'll see." She parks the car in front of a playground.
The chains on the swings are twisted and look as if
they haven't been touched in years. There isn't grass.
There's tan woodchips and a small dirt pile by the
merry-go-round. A red broken condom is lying beside
the jungle gym. There are no houses, and the playground
is like an island in the middle of a small town.
"Here?" I say to her before I get out of the car.
Alexis nods. "Yes. His parents don't think we should be
together. Black girl, white dude. Doesn't work."
"Why can't he come to our neighborhood? Your mom

wouldn't care." "But everyone else would. I can't walk down the street with him. No way." Alexis gets out of the car and fixes her clothes. She puts on grape lip gloss before she walks into the playground. Brandon comes from behind a bush and smiles. They hug and sit down together on the merry-go-round. It's just them. On their own little island. Their black and white playground.

An Invisible Wall

Nathan Hubel
First Place for High School Prose, 2011

A world of snow greeted me as I woke up at 6:30 a.m. only to find out that school was canceled. It was, I thought, going to be a great day. It was neither the winter wonderland nor even the closing of school I looked forward to so much as the ability to earn substantial amounts of money shoveling snow. Bundled up in several layers of winter clothing and with my oversized shovel in hand, I was ready to take on this snowed-in world. Most teenagers can make money shoveling in their neighborhoods, but mine is a gold mine. Much of the population is wealthy, elderly, and unfortunately, as I would soon find out, includes some racists.

By noon I was no longer quite as self-confident. I had underestimated the amount of effort it would take to shovel over a foot of snow in a reasonable amount of time. I did not have the build for this type of labor, and I was tiring quickly. However, I had finished four houses by noon and amassed an impressive $120 for the effort. Due to variables that affected the difficulty of the job from house to house, I allowed people to decide what they wanted to pay me. It was risky, but it paid off. When I finished with the fourth house and went to the owner for payment she said, "I usually only give $25 for shoveling, but since you worked so hard and you're from around here, I'll give you $30." I had never met this person before, but I assumed that she had seen me running near her house sometime, which I often had done.

I headed toward the next house that was buried in snow. As I was walking, I saw a number of other people wearing heavy black jackets and carrying huge shovels in the hopes of finding work. Some looked like professionals while others were about the same age and build as me, but from a distance everyone looked virtually identical. Two of the people walking towards me looking for houses to shovel were black, and I recognized them. They played basketball at the local high school in the adjacent neighborhood that I ran through in my training for cross-country. As I was walking past them, one of them asked, "Hey! How much you making around here?"

I replied, "About $30," which was the average for the four houses I had visited.

The first one looked surprised while the other one whistled loudly and asked rhetorically, "Why can't we get that much?"

"I think you know why. Forget this place, man," the first one responded with a mixture of sarcasm and anger. He turned to walk with his friend in the opposite direction. They were both stronger than I was, and thus probably did a better and faster job, but they obviously had gotten paid less for it. The sad thing was that I was not stunned.

Naturally, I hesitated to label those living in my neighborhood as racist, but after shoveling a few more houses and making similar amounts of money, I considered the possibility further. Having been a part of a local Boy Scout troop for a brief time, I had always known my neighborhood to be very provincial and to practice local favoritism. If I had gone up and asked the neighbors who paid the black shovelers unjustly, not to mention the strong possibility that some denied them work altogether because of the color of their skin, I have a strong suspicion that some would have responded, "They weren't from around here."

This does not make the actions of these neighbors any more excusable. Of course the black shovelers were from around here—just on the other side of a major roadway, one of many physical barriers in Pittsburgh conveniently separating racial communities from each other.

I cannot distinguish whether the injustice that the black shovelers experienced was pure racism or local favoritism superimposed with a racial element, but what I can point out is that even over fifty years after Martin Luther King led the movement for social equality and school integration, there is still a stunning lack of geographic integration between races. The reasons for this are multifaceted, as many people justifiably prefer living in the neighborhood they grew up in, feel most comfortable in, or can economically afford. But there are racist elements that seek to prevent the racial mixing of neighborhoods and forces that facilitate poverty in neighborhoods populated by underrepresented minorities. The sheer lack of diversity in many neighborhoods cannot be overlooked as a heavy contributor and indicator of the continued existence of racial prejudice.

The racial seclusion and division in many neighborhoods became all the more clear to me when my family had to go through the taxing process of moving to a new house. In one particular neighborhood that we researched online, there was a large crumbling wall covered in ivy. Two houses on one side of the wall cost around $200,000, but three houses of approximately equal size a few blocks away on the other side of the wall cost around $90,000. That side of the wall was a largely black neighborhood. The wall, now in complete disrepair, was a holdover from the pre-civil rights days when white communities built physical structures in order to separate communities.

Any defender of this seemingly inexplicable price difference might claim that the other house is "in a worse school district" or "in a less safe neighborhood," using numbers to justify lower property value. However, these claims are only true because people have created the conditions for it to be true. School districts tend to be based on these physical barriers and money is allocated unequally. Gangs and violence are directly correlated with unemployment and underemployment, which is also correlated with the quality of the school district one is born into.

Martin Luther King once said that he hopes to "look to a day when people will not be judged by the color of their skin, but by the content of their character." However, social injustices held over from the pre-civil rights days are still surreptitiously preventing the complete demise of racial injustice. Were the black shovelers paid less because people in my neighborhood assumed they were used to making less money than I was? What if I had accompanied the black shovelers that one snowy day? Would we have made the same amount of money per house that I did alone? Would it be assumed that I was not from the neighborhood, or would it be assumed that the black shovelers were from the neighborhood? Either way, while physical walls separating white and black neighborhoods have long since crumbled, invisible psychological barriers still remain.

Phone Bank

Amanda Huminski
Third Place for High School Prose, 2004

I am the only white female in this small training room. The women around me—45, 50, and black—talk about their children and other jobs. It is 5:00, we've just arrived, and we're all tired. In cubicles all around us there are voices rising and falling in gentle pistons of introductions and rebuttals. We learn how to make people like us for twenty minutes and forget our names as they hang up.

I have never worked like this before. I have never worked before. I imagine my first paycheck swollen with possibilities. All of theirs meager, barely filling their stomachs. Shredded by grocery shopping, rent, phone bills, cigarettes.

We fill out forms. My last name is longer than any of theirs and I claim the least tax exemptions. At break, a woman tells me that her son, who was about my age and a beast on the mic, was shot in the back of the head last year.

"I can only work fifteen hours a week," another woman says, "or else they'll cut back my welfare."

My mother held us in this balance once and my father took us away. But today, for the second time in my life, I see the scales wavering again on a survival point. My colleagues, my peers, sit around me making phone calls. I did not fight for my job. I could not support a family from this seat.

Things I Know about Rhinoceros

Amanda Huminski
Honorable Mention for High School Poetry, 2003

Rhinoceros have bad eyesight.
Rhinoceros are easily angered.
Rhinoceros come in two varieties, white and black.
        Maybe this next fact is true,
        and maybe it's not so true,
        but I've heard that the real difference
        isn't their color at all.
        I remember hearing somewhere
        that the difference was in their mouths.
        Not their hides,
        or even their temper or eyes.
        The white rhino has a flat upper lip.
        The black rhino has a pointed one.
        My source says that in the early days
        of safaris and khaki shorts,
        somebody misheard the word white instead of wide.
        The wide-lipped rhino became the white rhino
        and, because everybody knows
        that the opposite of white is black,
        the other became the black rhino.
        Or at least that's what I've heard.
Rhinoceros are a lot like humans.
        Not because they lumber around
        barely seeing their surroundings
        and charging at things that rustle in the bushes,
        but because they're separated,
        labels based on faulty names given by mistake.
The last thing I know about Rhinoceros,
        you can get a better look at them
        in a museum, stuffed and dead.

What *Really* Happened

Rachel Jardini
Second Place for High School Poetry, 2006

Every time I try to write
this poem about racism
I get this far
but erase what I have
because I am worried
that it might be offensive.

I am worried
because I know
that the stereotypes
are based on truth.

I hate that this is a common problem
and that the truth is worse
than the lies we use to hide it
and that we are ashamed.

I want to write a poem
about my black brother in jail,
about the smart Asian in my math class,
about the Mexican girl on welfare,
about the Iraqi man who blew up a train,
and about the white lawyers with SUVs.

I am tempted to start over
and write a poem
about the new student in our class
from a country we had never heard of
whom we befriended,

because I am the only one who will know
that we never actually talked to her
because her accent was weird.

I am tempted not to write
this poem about racism at all
but I know that this
cannot be left unsaid.
I am tempted to find that girl

whose name was foreign to us.
But that doesn't matter
because we never took the time
to say her name correctly
or to get to know
what else defined her
besides her foreign name
and her olive-colored skin.
I wish I could find her and ask
what *really* happened.

Letters

Leo Johnson
Second Place for High School Poetry, 2013

J, I never learned to spell your name,
to write the Hindi in Latin letters.
It seems an appalling omission now:
three years of friendship,
a fourth of obsession and
I never learned to spell your name.

Then again, I was younger then.
I couldn't spell "cinnamon."
While you were learning to write formal essays,
I couldn't spell the words to make you
look at me again,
draw for me again,
write for me again,
play four square with me again.
Two years seems like such a small difference now.
We were younger then.
You were the first girl I fell in love with.

It seems silly now:
Chinese Checkers in the after-school program
(I wonder now if it's wrong to call it that),
and my mother was late to pick me up.
I don't remember what I saw in you then.
Maybe it was just that you were nice.
You played with me; most people wouldn't.
I was so often too shy to speak.

You, the only dark-skinned student in your grade;
you, one of five nonwhite kids in the six hundred,
a fraction: one over one hundred and twelve,
less than one percentage point.

You must have known what it was to be an outsider.
I never knew how to have a friend before you.
You taught me holding hands,
sharing favorite books or websites or foods,
playdates not arranged by parents.

Two outsiders don't make one friendship,
two unmatched halves don't make one whole.
I didn't know what was different about me then,
I'm only beginning to understand now.
You couldn't not know what was different about you.
You were the first girl I fell in love with.
Trapped in this girl's body, this wrong body,
I didn't realize it for years, but I fell in love with you:
you whose mother put a bindi on my head,
you whose kitchen I ate meatloaf in for the first time.
I fell in love with you in your dark living room,
watching you as you watched Teen Titans.

You gave me a nickname,
you chose my first name after my birth name,
my much despised birth name, now traded in.
Those first nicknames, love names:
I was Chandni, in Hindi, moon.
You were Tara, in Hindi, star.

I begged you to draw pictures for me,
I begged you to write stories for me,
I begged you to play tag with me,
later I begged you not to leave me.
My first breakup: fourth grade.
You were never cruel, but again and again,
you weren't there when I looked for you in the halls.
Did you ever read those desperate, cursive letters,
the ones I left folded for you on the counter
of the afters-chool day care program?

I hope you didn't.
My desperation seems embarrassing in retrospect,
your eagerness to grow up all too understandable.
I think that maybe, if we were older,
these things could have been handled.
But what others would have risen in their places?

Lesbo. Psycho. Bulldyke. Creepy.
Those were the next names others gave me.
I don't know what they called you,
if they ever called you names.
You never told me.

I don't know if you called me those yourself,
when you grew up,
when you moved on,
when you made friends who weren't
desperate, alone, queer, younger, scared, crazy.
I want to think you never called me names.
It might be too much to ask
(I don't think I'd blame you if you did).

If I knew how to spell your name
maybe I could send you a letter.
Not this one, but a letter.
J: the one letter I am sure of.
One J isn't enough to find someone.
Would you want to be found if I could?
This poem is the last letter
that I will ever write to you.

Blasian

Taylor Johnson
Second Place for High School Poetry, 2012 (Tie)

When I was in
fourth grade, I
liked to be alone.
Hugging my knees
tight, pretending.
The boys,
wrestling on the brick,
the girls, in their corners,
giggling and blushing
behind tight hands.
Me, the observer.
Legs dangling from the stone.
I noticed that all
the black girls
were huddled together.
Then I look to the other side
of the playground.
All the white girls were
also together, playing with
sidewalk chalk.
This was the first time
I became aware of
the difference between
little black
girls &
little white
girls.
They taught us in school
that Martin Luther King
saved us. That he
stopped
segregation. As much as I want to
believe
that, I couldn't.
In art class, later that day,
we were learning our
warm
and
cool colors.
A new girl came in our class,

the principal by her side,
and her head held high.
Her skin was brown like
a toasted almond.
They put her right
next to me.
She had no supplies,
she just listened that period.

As the bell was ringing,
I was putting my things into my Bratz backpack.
She came over to me and asked,
"Are you Chinese or something?
I thought Chinese people didn't go here."
My little heart pounded
in my chest.
I shook my head so
hard at her.
Every bone in me
wanted not to be Chinese.
I felt myself on the verge of
tears, washing out of my
Chinese eyes.
I tried opening them bigger,
as big as they could go
just to prove to her.
I would not be Chinese.

I was always told I had
lighter skin than most people.
I asked my friend,
if I looked Chinese, and she told me
"You aren't Chinese? I thought you
were Blasian!"

What is Blasian?
Was that a real race?
I didn't want to be Blasian.
I wanted to be black,
like all the other
little black girls.

Letter from Indian Country

Katy June-Friesen
First Place for College Prose, 2004

"These people with all this land, eh?" says my mechanic, Larry. We're riding in his truck through the desert north of Albuquerque, New Mexico, along the shadow of Sandia Mountain. He drops me off at the Santa Ana Pueblo reservation and says, bueno, he'll have my car ready by noon.

For the past year, my work has been here—on Pueblo land, where Americans for Indian Opportunity (AIO) rents an office from the Santa Ana tribe.

Officially, I'm an AmeriCorps VISTA volunteer and the public information associate for AIO. More accurately, I've been a guest in a national Native community focused on bringing Indigenous voices to local, national, and international affairs. I consider my job with AIO a privilege because I arrived as a cultural outsider and became a collaborator.

My experience in this five-person office might be compared to a non–Mennonite entering a Mennonite community. There are last names, foods, inside humor, traditions, and gatherings that one must get to know.

So I've attended Pueblo feast days, where visitors are invited to eat in Pueblo members' homes, and the ceremonies honor a specific Catholic saint. On these visits, I've watched ceremonial dances, become familiar with traditional Pueblo regalia and learned the finer points of red and green chile, beans, oven bread, bread pudding, enchiladas, and potato salad.

In the AIO office, I've read tribal and national Native newspapers, followed tribal elections, learned about casinos, federal government policies, economic development, tribal governments, and trust lands. I've also written press releases and edited the AIO newsletter.

When I was in grade school, I dressed up as an Indian for Thanksgiving every other year. On the off years, I was a pilgrim. In third grade, our class had an "Indians Unit." I remember going to Sand Prairie, west of Newton, Kansas, and examining the plants the Plains Indians used to survive. We studied the "artifacts" of their culture and put up teepees; we didn't learn about the impact of colonization on Native communities.

Now I know about the year 1598, sixty years after the Spanish first arrived in the Southwest, when expedition leader Don Juan de Oñate declared all Pueblo people subjects of the Spanish monarch. At Acoma Pueblo, the warriors refused to submit to the declaration and killed thirteen Spanish soldiers. In response, the Spanish army killed hundreds of Acoma people and amputated one foot of each of the male prisoners who were over the age of twenty-five.

More importantly, I now understand how the histories of colonization connect to the present and how Native peoples were able to survive and move on. For example, when the Spanish didn't leave the Southwest, Pueblo people learned to shroud native religion in Catholicism to appease the Spanish throne and used Catholic holy days to practice traditional ways.

This kind of creative response still lives today in Native communities across the nation, as members participate in both their traditional culture and contemporary society. I've met people who are active in federal institutions and traditional tribal governments, tribes and non-native communities, urban law firms and rural economic development initiatives, language preservation projects and the Bureau of Indian Affairs, traditional drumming and singing groups, and Native reggae bands. They have learned to make many worlds work as one.

In May—as the United States was bombing the land and people of Iraq with promises of liberation—sovereignty over land and culture took on another layer of meaning. I attended a celebration at Sandia Pueblo for legislation recently signed into law to protect Sandia Mountain.

The mountain is sacred to the people of Sandia Pueblo. They have lived in a community at its base, thirteen miles north of Albuquerque, for the past seven hundred years and have maintained ownership of most of the mountain's western face.

The legislation is a result of collaboration and long negotiation with New Mexico congressional representatives, the federal government, and an area homeowners' group. The new law allows Sandia Pueblo to regain control of Sandia Mountain land that was excluded from its control by a now invalid 1859 U.S. Interior Department survey.

Pueblo member J. R. Trujillo explained the importance of the new legislation: "We always face the Mountain when we pray. It is just like an altar to us . . . where we greet the sun coming out. We do believe that the spirit is there that will grant us all our lives. After all, it's the spirit that any nation, any people, believe in, and it's the spirit that gives life."

In a time when the United States is engaged in the violence of empire-building abroad, I am glad to have driven under the shadow of Sandia Mountain every day on my way to work, along the Rio Grande, where Native communities still live today.

Coloring Book

Justin Ker
Honorable Mention for College Poetry, 2003

I once tried to color an Indian
blue
and discovered
that my own skin was yellow.

This was fifteen years ago in Singapore—
my art teacher shook her head
and plucked the fat blue crayon
from the smallness of my hands.

I can still smell the crushed pastels,
the sweet smear of crayon on my thumb,
staining the memory of my fingers.

She looked at my incomplete coloring
of the four smiling figures,
standing shoulder to shoulder,
our little flag of political correctness that also showed
the tension in its threads.
The slant eyes behind the bespectacled Chinese face,
the big nose, curly hair of the Indian,
the Eurasian with his hybrid features—
eyes from Austria between his Asian ears.
And the Malay, standing at the far right,
almost at the picture's edge,
marginalized in our little country,
as in a coloring book.

The artist drew in these subtle clues,
etching them onto our young brains,
fearing that six-year-old boys with crayons
could not decipher
the colorless outlines.

My art teacher pointed to the drawing
of the smiling turbaned man
and handed me the brown crayon—
this is for the Indian.
My wrist moved over the paper,
shading in his arms, his face—

his life story, in which he gets drunk
every night on the cheapest beer
and comes home at 4 a.m. to beat his wife.
She, for one, is glad for her dark Indian skin—
the bruises are not *that* obvious.

And so it is with the Malay,
eventually a cleaner, a chauffeur,
a moral of the story against laziness,
for the master narrative of the Chinese.

And the Eurasian?
"Just mix any of the colors," she said.
This, a primitive exercise in gene recombination
for a six-year-old god with crayons.

Fifteen years later in Pittsburgh,
I am tired of the wasted metaphors
about color and race,
in a country where the man who steals your stereo
must be black,
where the man who steals your nuclear secrets
must be yellow.
It seems only the minorities are thieves.

But the black man isn't actually black—
his skin is a deep brown coded by some one hundred genes,
one hundred out of the forty thousand human ones,
and not one is a gene for stealing stereos.

We're so hung up on race,
trapped at these one hundred genes,
that it makes us incredibly stupid.

We wrap our bodies in the uncolored
double helix of ourselves,
surrounded by strands of skin color,
writing poems, flogging the PC carriage,
when all we need to do
is to let a six-year-old boy
color as he pleases.

A Different Kind of Field

Sierra Laventure-Voltz
First Place for High School Prose, 2004

Racism never falters in the eyes of the young. Children grow to be as their parents would have them become, and the cycle repeats itself with every generation. This natural occurrence cannot be changed by mere hope for a better world. As a child myself, I learned that the tables could be turned, that I was not so safely hidden from the world around me.

My first year at Winchester Thurston was seventh grade, and while being about halfway through the soccer season, I was only just starting to become comfortable with the people around me. Soccer made me exceptionally nervous, but when I look back on it now there was no reason for me to feel so pressured. A starting player, I always worked as hard as I could. Back then, however, all I could think about was making the mistake that would cost us the game. Every game made my body shake and my stomach churn; it terrified me that not only did my starting position lie in the path of my mistakes, but that I might lose the few friends I had made, simply because of a game.

Quiet and reserved, I always sat and talked with the few other girls on the team. I felt that if I said something or did something that displeased the boys, they would not play with me. I had no idea what real discrimination entailed, but I would soon learn.

After school, on a hot, late September afternoon, we changed into our gear for practice. Coach told us that we were traveling to a field we had never played on before. We did not know anything about the field except that it was a drive and that it was in the Hill District. Loading everything onto the bus, I grew excited. What an adventure this would be for me, the new girl.

On this particular ride, I sat near the front with my only real friend, Ugochi, whom I was always with. The trip to the field was about twenty minutes, but the last five minutes we drove through the heart of the Hill District. I had never been there before and was astonished at what I saw. My face glued to the window, I viewed poverty in a place I had never expected it to be, a half hour from my house. Crumbling buildings furnished with ragged banners hanging off of them, saying things such as, "Mike was killed by police officers when he was 13 years old," and, "Our suffering is not our fault."

Black men, women, and children walked through the ugly, potholed streets, sometimes wearing tattered clothing. My fear overrode my senses, and I could not speak. How, I asked myself, could people live like this? The obvious hatred I saw in this society sickened me. I had grown up sheltered from the racism, hardships, and poverty that some of our country is subjected to. Perhaps we never should have come here.

We pulled up to the field and as we walked up the hill towards it, I realized how poor this neighborhood really was. The trees were starting to turn to the beautiful autumn colors, yet the air was still heavy with humidity; I could smell fall. However, even this perfect day could not help brighten the atmosphere of the field. It was in shambles: a football field with no soccer goals at the ends and a chain link fence around the edge, barbed wire strung along the top of the fence. The yard lines were barely visible and the field goals rusted to the color of the changing leaves. We brought our backpacks from the bus and left them on the sidelines. Practice began normally, and we warmed up by running a lap around the field. Coach split us up into different teams and we started to play.

About halfway through practice, a few young boys, apparently from a football team, started to come from the entrance of the field to laze and sit behind our bags. Their interest in us led them to take a few of our soccer balls to play with. These boys were trying so hard to understand how to play, but they just could not handle the ball. Their uniforms were all black, but faded, and while scrawny and short, these boys looked tough and determined. Our team took a water break and one of the kids playing near us asked me how long our practice would last. I said that we would be gone around five-thirty and I ran off to play again.

A few minutes later, a large group of men appeared and walked onto the field. One of them, hard-faced with a cruel swagger, walked up to my father and started to bellow at him. He made it clear that he was the coach of the black kids' football team. My dad, the assistant coach of my team, did not know what to say, and, while backing away, he called for our head coach. We were spread out all over the field, but when we heard the yelling, we came over quickly. Coach told us to go on the end line and wait, but while we were walking off, the whole football team gathered around our coaches. The man in charge of the football team was screaming, "Get off our field!"

My coach put himself between the black man and my father. I looked back quickly at the dark storm brewing around my coaches before I ran over to watch intently with Ugochi.

Coach spoke softly, but sternly. "There must have been a mistake. I called and I have a permit for this field at this time."

There were other coaches with the black kids, or perhaps they were parents who shared the same feelings as their coach. The men added to the commotion. The head football coach screamed, "This is our field! We always practice on this field and will always practice on this field! GET OFF!"

As Coach gave up the fight, he put his hands out a little, motioning that he meant no harm. He told us to grab our bags quickly and get on the bus. We filed out, but while we were all squeezing through the gate, a man stood to the side with a hard hat on. He was one of the men with the football coach. Studying each one of us individually as we walked by, he looked interested. He asked what school we were from, and it seemed that I was the only one who could answer, "Winchester Thurston." The man nodded and looked at me strangely. I knew he had no idea where our school was, but he thought it was important to act like he did.

I remember having Ugochi next to me, thinking how she felt about what had just happened. Her parents were from Nigeria, and I wanted to know if she felt uncomfortable that she had been put into the racial group of the rich and the white. I would never know; I was too scared and embarrassed to ask.

At the bottom of the hill, a girl I was walking next to exclaimed that she had left her backpack on the field. She was carrying the ball bag, and since I had some extra energy, I told her that I would go retrieve it for her. I got to her backpack, but as I walked back off the field, I noticed that some of the same football kids who had been so friendly earlier were staring at me. I tried not to look at them and kept walking straight. All of a sudden, I heard some of the kids on the field start to yell, "That's right, white girl, get off our field! This place is ours, white girl!"

Their coaches stood nearby watching, saying nothing. The jeering did not end until my coach walked up to me from the entrance. I was about ten yards away from the kids and still on the field when Coach said to me, "That was the right thing to do. Just keep your head held high and they can't touch you. Always be proud."

The bus ride back to school was filled with complaining about the "psycho" coach who had kicked us off "their" field. We did not see what must have been too obvious for him. The whites had come to stake claim to his field, much like what happened to his neighborhood in the past. I now see his predicament, and do not blame him for what he did, for he felt threatened. He must have grown up with the idea that white people want to take everything from him, and for him this was true. The Hill District used to thrive with black culture, and now it is fading as a neighborhood. The most heart-wrenching thing is that he was a role model for the children that he coached. They looked up to him, and I am sure they felt proud that he had chased us from the field. Those children will grow to be as closed-minded as he.

My coach, with his words, taught me not only that I could be strong in the face of fear but also that pride can be a double-edged sword. Did not the children have pride in their coach who threw us from the field? But was he correct in his actions? Simply because you believe in what you are doing does not mean that it is your right to act upon your feelings. Sometimes my mind wanders back to that day, and I think about how irrelevant school, classes, and sports are compared to the real world events going on around me. Toleration cannot be taught by others. Only by experience and understanding can the transformation occur. I learned a great deal at a young age about what is truly important and what stands superfluously on the outskirts of life.

Sushi at Yunioshi's

Kevin Lee
First Place for College Poetry, 2016

You probably think you've seen me
sipping bubble teas, walking Pekingese
and other small breeds across these city streets
kicking it with Mr. Miyagi in the back seat
of my Honda Accord SE, puffin' poppy seeds
bumpin' Far East, and always acting accordingly.
I'm that young Bruce Lee with the buckteeth
and Coke-bottle frames,
that don't know he don't know how to sing.
But you know I know when that "Hotrine Bring"
I'm that Karaoke King with that four-inch thing.
I'm that chink in the back pew
trading Yu-Gi-Oh cards for Pikachu.
I'm that dude with the kimchi stains
on his Canada-Goose-Fu-Manchu,
dripping down to his Jimmy Choo shoes.
For some reason,
I'm not the person you know but the guy that you see.
But if you ever want to get to know the real me,
I'll be sippin' soju like it's iced tea
on the corner of Mott Street
eating sushi with Mr. Yunioshi.

Half Smile

Tyler Lewis
Second Place for College Poetry, 2002

I, at one time, loved my color—
It opened sMALL doors of tokenism & acceptance.
—Haki Madhubuti "The Self-Hatred of Don L. Lee"

Some kid I tutored called me
a sellout,
        said I talked funny.
I kinda smiled, I'd heard it before.
Many times. He was only ten.
I didn't know what to say.

            I used to love my color.
Perhaps for the tokenism? Perhaps not?
That little validation protected me
      from the white hoods
           from the broken bottles
               thrown at heads.

I was twelve when I saw someone
shot walking to the 7-Eleven.
      Bullet grazed my ear.
Nigga on the ground. Momma decided
to ship me off to a better place.
That is too vague a reason,

         you know?
Once there, I began to love the me
that didn't court trouble. The me
that made them more comfortable.
      I cried my eyes
         out every time
            I didn't defend myself.

I remember the streets of my youth.
It is not enough to say I've gotten out.
      Life only seems good.
I sit by a window. The kid next to me.
I could have told him all this.
But I sit there, kinda smile. He knew.

Finding the Perfect American Model

Ang Li
Honorable Mention for High School Prose, 2004

Many times, I wished that I had been born here so I wouldn't have to try so hard to mold myself into an American. I would be one naturally. For years, I searched for the perfect American model. I watched my classmates, spied on my neighbors, and surveyed the people on the PAT bus. But no matter how hard I searched, I never found her.

I was brought up to believe that as long as I am the best at my studies, everything else would take care of itself. In China, the kid with the perfect grades is the teacher's pride. I was that pride. As a way to indulge in their pride, the teachers granted me special privileges. That was how I became the president of the class without having any leadership abilities. Being a class officer never meant service to me; it meant being the focus of respect. Our fifth grade was a little hierarchy, and I was clearly the queen. Every kid revered me in fear of me marking crosses beside their names. That was my job, to mark crosses on the name list if a kid's fingernail was dirty, or if he forgot to bring pencils to class. Hello Kitty pencils and pretty erasers flooded my way. I was spoiled to think that I would always be popular.

I carried my haughtiness across the ocean with me. In my ESL class of twenty people, I made a friend the first day of school. When a Taiwanese girl came up to me and introduced herself as Pauline, I thought it was just my innate charisma that attracted her attention. I didn't try to impress her. When she gave me a Pikachu keychain, I didn't feel obliged to give anything back to her. I never learned how to pay my share of friendship. I learned quickly and became the best in the ESL class. But for the first time, being the best in my class didn't get me all that I wanted. A part of me longed for compliments. When a new girl joined our class, Pauline began to gradually abandon me. When she was sure of her position in the new girl's heart, she ignored me for good. I blamed her poor judgment. I would have made many friends just to make her jealous, but I didn't know how. Pauline took away my haughtiness for good.

When I got into a real American school, I became careful then. I became introverted, not trusting my personality. Though I didn't figure out exactly why Pauline disliked me, I began to think that I was the one at fault. I rarely spoke in school in fear of Americans thinking me mentally challenged because of my broken English. I fled from the populated lounge to a library corner to hide my Chinese ways. I went under the pretext of studying, but sometimes I just wanted a place to talk to myself. I blushed over every mispronunciation. "Close the light, please," I would venture to say, and then realize my mistake. At such moments I wished people would see the advanced calculus I was doing in math or the full credit on my last history exam so that they would know that I was actually pretty smart.

After a while, I gave up speaking. I rarely showed my teeth. I didn't want anyone to know that my parents couldn't afford braces. "Sorry," was one of the few words

I uttered. I would say it repeatedly when I stepped on someone's shoe—not because I was overly apologetic, but because I was afraid of others thinking me unkind.

I often cried in my room. I didn't want to talk to my parents because they wouldn't understand why I was so depressed when I was getting straight As. I couldn't write about my frustration to friends in China because I was too proud to let them know that their perfect president was struggling over trifling matters like making new American friends. Instead, I told them about the cozy library in my American school. I told them the title of the first English book I read: *Charlie and the Chocolate Factory.* I wondered why I had things to hide. Many kids would have given up everything to come to America. All those articles I've read in China about Chinese immigrants showed such a different experience from what I was going through. It was supposed to be a good time, and I was supposed to be the happiest kid in the world.

Before I came here, I dreamed about all the American stuff I would own. But reality is always ironic. The few new clothes we bought all had tags that said made in China. Mom shuddered at the thought that every dollar spent is eight yuans lost. "That's crazy! A backpack costs a hundred bucks!" She would frown after multiplying the price by eight. Mom kept reminding me that if we saved enough, we could go back to Ji Nan one day and be millionaires and have shopping sprees all the time. I didn't think that day was coming soon.

Once in English class, I was called upon to make a comment. I don't remember much about the question or what I answered. But the part I do remember stuck to me. It was the first time I spoke during class. Though I was blushing, I knew I wasn't doing too badly. But all of a sudden, I heard giggles. I didn't realize the kids were laughing at me until I finished my comment and thought hard about everything I'd said. It had become my habit—to think both before and after talking. That was when I realized I'd said "sky scratchers." I thought it made sense. The buildings are so tall that they scratch the sky. But it didn't sound right. It sounded like the wooden hand grandpa used when his back itched. I prayed that not too many people caught my malapropism. I was too occupied with embarrassment to ask the correct name for tall buildings.

I read books out loud at home. I spoke to myself in English before going to sleep. I marked my textbooks with Chinese translations. Eventually, my English became better. Though I only spoke when I was absolutely sure, I opened my mouth more often. But it was after an instant's revelation that I finally opened up.

I joined a summer class called Andrew's Leap for high school kids at Carnegie Mellon University. The school is a gathering of many nationalities. I watched the foreign college kids, wanting to find anybody having the same problems as I did. I was surprised to find none. Though some of them apparently weren't fluent either, they composed themselves comfortably in front of Americans. I felt sorry for myself. For a while, I was beginning to think that I would never belong. No matter how good my English was getting, I could never be free. I saw my future lying in front of me: a lifetime of hiding behind a desperate mask to please, a life of silence and a closed mouth. But the bit of pride that was left in me began to rebel. I wondered why these kids felt more comfortable with themselves than I did when my English, though not perfect, was better than theirs. There was a tiny voice in my head that shouted out for attention, "If they can do it, why can't you?" I was pressured to join conversations just to prove to that voice that I was not a coward.

Then I realized that I didn't need to prove it to anyone, not even that little voice in my head. Now, I know who I am and that is whom I should present. I don't need to be hypocritical to be nice to people. I don't need to hide.

I started to realize that no one, except myself, minded my mispronunciations; no one, but myself, was embarrassed by my Chinese ways. In fact, when I started to pay attention to the outside world, I found out that many American kids chose to learn Chinese. I found out that Chinese food is the most popular choice for advisee lunch. I started to use chopsticks again after a girl asked me to teach her how to pick up rice using just two sticks.

I found out that it's not so deplorable to add an extra "s" on the ends of words. I began to talk. No only in English, but in Chinese as well. When I'm overly excited, I let slip a "wo dee tian ah" and take pleasure in the fact that no one else knows what I mean. I say the multiplication table in Chinese and get my answers faster than using a calculator. When my classmates stare at me in amazement, I say, "It's a Chinese thing." When some kid tried to be cool and said, "Nee How," I told him that it's a cheap American imitation and taught him the native way to say hello. I laughed with him when even I got confused with the tricky nasal vowels.

Some Americans like to drink coffee in the morning while others prefer milk and cereal. I eat a scrambled egg. While the rest of America is split between Pepsi and Coke, I love velvet corn soup more than any soda. All of my classmates are practicing their superstar signatures; I found mine being the most unique because I sign it in Chinese. I had tried so hard to be an American without knowing that there isn't even a consistent model for me to follow. So in the end, I accepted my own differences. Now that I think about it, it was a very American choice. After all, America is a mosaic of differences where one can be whoever she wants to be.

I never had trouble academically. I was never disliked by a teacher. I rarely made people mad at me. In many ways, one can say that I have an easy life. But it was what others take for granted I lacked. I struggled for years finding a perfect model of American ways so I can mold myself into her. During these years, I've learned how to solve an integral of a function over an infinite interval; what terrifying things the Jacobins did during the French revolution; why a ball falls straight down even though the earth is moving; how much linseed oil to mix with turpentine to create the perfect medium for oil painting. However, if one were to ask what's the most important thing I've learned, I don't need time to choose among all these things. I would say that the most important thing I've learned is to be my own model.

Fighting a Forbidden Battle: How I Stopped Covering Up for a Hidden Wrong

Jesse Lieberfeld
First Place for High School Prose, 2012 (Tie)

I once belonged to a wonderful religion. I belonged to a religion that allows those of us who believe in it to feel that we are the greatest people in the world . . . and feel sorry for ourselves at the same time. Once, I thought that I truly belonged in this world of security, self-pity, self-proclaimed intelligence, and perfect moral aesthetic. I thought myself to be somewhat privileged early on. It was soon revealed to me, however, that my fellow believers and I were not part of anything so flattering.

Although I was fortunate enough to have parents who did not try to force me into any one set of beliefs, being Jewish was in no way possible to escape growing up. It was constantly reinforced at every holiday, every service, and every encounter with the rest of my relatives. I was forever reminded how intelligent my family was, how important it was to remember where we had come from, and to be proud of all the suffering our people had overcome in order to finally achieve their dream in the perfect society of Israel.

This last mandatory belief was one I never fully understood, but I always kept the doubts I had about Israel's spotless reputation to the back of my mind. "Our people" were fighting a war, one I did not fully comprehend, but I naturally assumed that it must be justified. We would never be so amoral as to fight an unjust war. Yet as I came to learn more about our so-called "conflict" with the Palestinians, I grew more concerned. I routinely heard about unexplained mass killings, attacks on medical bases, and other alarmingly violent actions for which I could see no possible reason. "Genocide" almost seemed the more appropriate term, yet no one I knew would have ever dreamed of portraying the war in that manner; they always described the situation in shockingly neutral terms. Whenever I brought up the subject, I was always given the answer that there were faults on both sides, that no one was really to blame, or simply that it was a "difficult situation."

It was not until eighth grade when I fully understood what I was on the side of. One afternoon, after a fresh round of killings was announced on our bus ride home, I asked two of my friends who actively supported Israel what they thought. "We need to defend our race," they told me. "It's our right."

"We need to defend our race."

Where had I heard that before? Wasn't it the same excuse our own country had used to justify its abuses of African Americans sixty years ago? In that moment, I realized how similar the two struggles were—like the white radicals of that era, we controlled the lives of another people whom we abused daily, and no one could speak out against us. It was too politically incorrect to do so. We had suffered too much, endured too many hardships, and overcome too many losses to be criticized. I realized then that I was in no way a part of a "conflict"—the term "Israeli/Palestinian Conflict" was no more accurate than calling the Civil Rights Movement the "Caucasian/African American Conflict." In both cases, the expression was a blatant euphemism: it gave the impression that this was a dispute among equals and that both held an equal share of the blame. However, in both, there was clearly an oppressor and the oppressed, and I felt horrified at the realization that I was by nature on the side of the oppressors. I was grouped with the racial supremacists. I was part of a group that killed while praising its own intelligence and reason. I was part of a delusion.

I thought of the leader of the other oppressed side of years ago: Martin Luther King. He too had been part of a struggle that had been hidden and glossed over for the convenience of those against whom he fought. What would his reaction have been? As it turned out, it was precisely the same as mine. As he wrote in his letter from Birmingham Jail, he believed the greatest enemy of his cause to be "Not the White Citizen's Council-er or the Ku Klux Klan-er, but the white moderate, who . . . lives by a mythical concept of time. . . . Lukewarm acceptance is much more bewildering than outright rejection."

When I first read those words, I felt as if I were staring at myself in a mirror. All my life I had been conditioned to simply treat the so-called conflict with the same apathy that King had so forcefully condemned. I, too, held the role of an accepting moderate. I, too, "lived by a mythical concept of time," shrouded in my own surreal world and the set of beliefs that had been assigned to me. I had never before felt so trapped.

I decided to make one last appeal to my religion. If it could not answer my misgivings, no one could. The next time I attended a service, there was an open question-and-answer session about any point of our religion. I wanted to place my dilemma in as clear and simple terms as I knew how. I thought out my exact question over the course of the seventeen-minute cello solo that was routinely played during service. Previously, I had always accepted this solo as just another part of the program, yet now it seemed to capture the whole essence of our religion: intelligent and well-crafted on paper, yet completely oblivious to the outside world (the soloist did not have the faintest idea of how masterfully he was putting us all to sleep).

When I was finally given the chance to ask a question, I asked, "I want to support Israel. But how can I when it lets its army commit so many killings?"

I was met with a few angry glares from some of the older men, but the rabbi answered me. "It is a terrible thing, isn't it?" he said. "But there's nothing we can do. It's just a fact of life."

I knew, of course, that the war was no simple matter and that we did not by any means commit murder for its own sake, but to portray our thousands of killings as a "fact of life" was simply too much for me to accept. I thanked him and walked out shortly afterward. I never went back. I thought about what I could do. If nothing else, I could at least try to free myself from the burden of being saddled with a belief I could not hold with a clear conscience. I could not live the rest of my life as one of the pathetic moderates whom King had rightfully portrayed as the worst part of the problem. I did not intend to go on being one of the Self-Chosen People, identifying myself as part of a group to which I did not belong.

It was different not being the ideal nice Jewish boy. The difference was subtle, yet by no means unaffecting. Whenever it came to the attention of any of our more religious family friends that I did not share their beliefs, I was met with either a disapproving stare and a quick change of the subject, or an alarmed cry of, "What? Doesn't Israel matter to you?" Relatives talked down to me more afterward, but eventually I stopped noticing the way adults around me perceived me. It was worth it to no longer feel as though I were just another apathetic part of the machine.

I obviously can never know what it must have been like to be an African American in the 1950s. I do feel, however, as though I know exactly what it must have been like to be white during that time, to live under an aura of moral invincibility, to hold unchallengeable beliefs, and to contrive illusions of superiority to avoid having to face simple everyday truths. That illusion was nice while it lasted, but I decided to pass it up. I have never been happier.

A Question Finally Answered

Shai Mallory
First Place for High School Poetry, 2003

Port Authority Transit (PAT),
that's what I use to go from here to there.
Tonya, Marquida, Kelly, and I
decided to take a long bus ride.

It was a hot summer day.
We were impatiently standing at the corner of Ross Street,
waiting on the PAT,
the one that said, 67A Monroeville Mall.

Tonya's cocoa skin shined from the sun.
Kelly, Marquida, and I are brown sugar.
If we stood in the sun any longer,
we were all likely to get a little darker.
Finally it pulled around the corner,
"Get y'all bus fare out, this is our bus."

We paid our fare and moved straight
to the back of the empty bus.
"See my days are cold without you . . ."
Tonya started singing. We all joined.
"But I'm hurting while I'm with you . . ."

Then I noticed an elderly white lady.
After paying her fare,
she stumbled to find a seat.
She was loaded with shopping bags,
she kept walking until she was sitting across from me.

This lady kept staring,
her eyes were filled with,
"I have a question."
Then finally she unlocked her jaws and said,
"Excuse me, if you don't mind my asking,
why do you choose to sit in the back of the bus
when your people fought so hard to
sit in the front?"

We were in shock,
as if we had run into an electric eel.

I don't think she knew how she made us feel.
So I leaned toward her,
to make sure she heard.
I said in a nice, but firm voice,
"Because now we have a choice."

The War on Terror

Kat Mandeville
Third Place for College Poetry, 2005

Without the Law a woman is as safe as the men allow her to be.
—Louis L'Amour

Dear Sir, to continue from the party, last night's
playful banter on inferiority and the sexes—
let us joke no more about men and women
and what really doesn't matter.

I know the strength of a woman. I've felt
my own impervious will—climb, fight,
move impossible things.

But I know the strength of a man—
the weight of a fallen tree
on a distracted traveler, I've had to gnaw
off a limb to recover the rest.

No, a woman is not helpless,
but don't let's pretend
her assets are your own.

When a dame says she sculpts and dresses
her body for herself, she means she is sharpening
her weapons, stocking her arsenal.

And we learned this in third grade, when the boys
went helpless to the first girl's grown breasts, forgetting
who she was, only what she could be.

And your goofy smirks and harmless slander
gave her permission to show more cleavage
and to turn away.

And this is her body
fighting back—
a tease protecting
the only real collateral.

Because she knows, deep down in places
we don't chat about at parties, that it is not

her mind—tear gas that clouds a room, leaves
a funny smell; it is not her ambition—which is
masculine anyway; it is not her credentials—
typed font ten just to fit all on the page,
not these obstacles—

it is the toss of her hair and the swing of her ass
that will save her life. That, as a commodity,
she must improve supply to increase demand,
raising her value into something like integrity,
and this is her only self-defense: to own
and distribute what everybody wants.
This is her pride—you love it
you want to tear it down.

So please, Sir, remember

that when you stroke my thigh without permission,
you are mocking the only cards I hold
in this lousy game.

That my leg is a blade

and when I watch your need and squeeze
your wrist, I'm admiring the mutilation,
how well you bleed.

That when aimed and cocked at your target,
half of us mean it and half of us don't,
and we all sound the same with the lights off.

That a woman without objection who follows you home
is only the weight of metal, with no bullets left
and she knows it.

Yoko

Sally Mao
Second Place for College Poetry, 2007

In the American schoolyard,
they chant their favorite rhymes again:
My mom is Chinese,
my dad is Japanese,
look what they did to me!
     They wedge their eyes up and down
into paisleys, yins & yangs,
and suddenly you are reminded of preschool
in Hunan, China, where the only face you remember
is Sheng Yoko, a half-Japanese classmate. She was
lovely, homesick.
     You had always secretly envied
the robin's-egg beads on her hair ties. The one time you shared
a bed with her at noontime nap, her hair smelled
like skim milk and sweet porridge, her pajamas
hand-washed, cleaner than yours. You stayed awake
wondering how it'd be to live in her house. Would it smell
like her? Or like apples and chives? Did she hear crickets
before her eyelids drooped at night?

     Then or now,
no matter how lovely their snow-covered gardens, how colorful
their origami paper, their watersilk costumes, nobody in your family
liked the Japanese. You were untouched,
yet you wanted to touch everyone—you were unsullied
by history—you didn't know how it flawed people, cultures,
how it coats pure landscapes with frictionless red.
Your family told you to stay away from her,

but that didn't stop you from complimenting her hand-painted
pencil box, her pearl-toothed comb, smiling at her
in those narrow spaces between unuttered secrets
and compulsory glances, where memory
can easily be erased. You were not
her friend. In this playground you don't remember
ever smiling.

Yoko was a pretty girl,
and though you did not know her,
you miss her so much.

RACEing in America

Anya Martin
Third Place for College Poetry, 2002

In my college dictionary, there are 24 definitions of race, beginning with obvious entries like #1: "a contest of speed, as in running, riding, driving or sailing," to #17: "a group of persons related by common descent or heredity." But then it becomes obscure with definitions like: "An urgent effort, as when a solution is imperative: 'a race to find a vaccine.'" And then you fall into the deep shit like #21: "a classification of modern humans, sometimes esp. formerly, based on arbitrary selections of physical characteristics, such as skin color, facial form, or eye shape, and now frequently based on genetic markers as blood groups. . . ."

You can't even read all the definitions before your mind is racing off to some romantic African plain where the natives compete barefoot, or maybe the Orient where the locals pedal through jungles filling their rice bowls, or even to German farmers sailing across the ocean to cut down trees and farm Indians' land. Maybe you don't know where the race begins, where the starting point is?

Home maybe?

Yes, I did hear my father tell a racist joke. But I was much smaller then and didn't get it. It had something to do with a black man on a boat with M&Ms—I can hardly remember. But jokes are a funny thing, see, because if you're a certain "color" or "heritage," you're allowed to tell some jokes, you know, like Chris Rock, but not everyone can do this.

It takes a long time to figure out which jokes are legal: how and when you're crossing the foul line. For I have laughed at sushi jokes, imitated all accents, like "Ghetto Slang," "Hispanic Taco," and "Redneck Hicks." But then there have been times when I didn't laugh, like in seventh grade at a Holocaust joke—something about raking ashes. I didn't think that was funny. But we all hear the starting gunshot at different times, sprinting out of blocks at varying speeds—speaking of which, I ran track in high school, and there were three black girls on the whole team. Damn, they were fast, but then they usually are—aren't they?

Now see, you're not supposed to make generalizations like that. For example, I have a foster sister whom I love: she's from Brooklyn, she's black—wait, not that everyone from Brooklyn is black (in fact a guy in my acting class is white and from Brooklyn)—but anyway, my foster sister is fat, and can't sing or run fast (although she does have soul, but then we all do, right?). That's one of those lines where we smile and agree that we're all the same. You see the red and yellow and black and white hands shaking, "Embrace Diversity!"

And embracing diversity is great until you bring another "race" home as your dinner date, then your mother, who may even teach first grade and have a similar poster with rainbow hands shaking in her classroom, suddenly sees that embracing diversity was taken a little too literally. Because you can be open-minded and still be a little racist, and sometimes that's even okay, because you can't deny the fact that there are "cultural" differences, and not admitting that you have them could be even worse. But how do you even know if you have "them," your prejudices? It's not an easy diagnosis to make or disease to cure, especially now that we are all politically correct.

Ever since I knew that it was bad to make "preconceptions" I've been trying not to. Yet I learned in Social Psychology that making generalizations and preconceptions are inherent to survival. If we thought out every situation and were open-minded about everything, then we might not live so long. For example, if someone comes in with a gun and points it at your head, and you analyze too long and ask too may questions about what's going on, then you'll probably end up dead. But then don't go categorizing all robbers, murders, and rapists as black, even though there is something like twice as many black convicts as white. But that's because of our racist system; it's all cyclical—being born into poverty leads to poverty. Yet, when I'm walking alone at night and two large black guys come up behind me, I must admit I get more nervous than if it were two white guys, even though I have been raped by a white man and seen poorer white people in my life than black or Hispanic. But this is not what this poem is about, because men are often assholes, all kinds, although the Spanish ones are more aggressive, so you need to be especially careful with them. Now you're thinking, "Oops, she messed up again, another gross generalization that is displaying her subconscious racism." That's what I would've thought too, until I worked in DC all summer, walking to work from Columbia Heights and praying not to get whistled or stared at, followed by the men on the street shouting, "Mamacita! Oooh!"

And I've tried to "help." I've spent entire summers in the "ghetto" teaching "underprivileged" children and teachers. I've made mission statements, I've corrected narrow-minded thinking among my friends and family, explaining words like "gentrification" and "self-fulfilling prophecy." I've been the only white person at poetry bars, rapped with seventh-grade black students, knowing full well that I have no rhythm. I can even manage to eat really spicy ethnic foods—Indian is my favorite. My roommate is Japanese and she's teaching me how to use chopsticks! I've been the righteous do-gooder, felt the white guilt heavy upon my shoulders, and at the same time relished patriotism for this great nation, racism and all. I have tried to believe in definition #20 of RACE: "the human race or family; humankind." But that's hard, too, since, God save us all, we hardly know what being human means, I mean there are seven definitions for "human" alone, not even taking into consideration all the things that being human entails, like love, hope, hate, fear, etc. I can't get my head around it. And I'd like to say that if we'd all just put our heads together, we could circle the colorful globe Embracing Diversity, like a love ring around Jupiter, and save the whales while we're at it. But I just don't know. . . .

You know?

For a Day the Air Is New

Claire Matway
First Place for High School Poetry, 2010

We trundle along in our yellow school bus,
eighth graders with the world
high above our heads. Hot sun
blows through our open windows
with the last breezes of spring, gloriously harsh light
on rough, potholed streets.
We're seated as usual:
a cluster of black kids in the rear, white kids
sprinkled along the middle, a few mixed groups in the front.
The day smells like new leaves and we
breathe it in.
Someone says,
"Hey!"
Here, a sudden shift in the atmosphere's texture! Here,
words move like paper airplanes: "Hey, you—
white kids! Come back here!" choruses
from the black kids in back, and
we turn around, grinning.
"Why're none of you back here? Come on!" they say.
The season changes
and it is time for our migration—
"Yeah, let's go!" we yell, and stumble through
the congested aisle, brown rubber of the seats
slick under our palms.
We smash in five to a seat,
shouting back and forth, exploding in laughter,
skin warm in the air.
Reorganize the layout, destroy the map! We are together for today;
if only for today, our own voices
have allowed us to break the rules.
When the bus' tires slow
against the gray of the road, we surge outside,
blinking sunlight into our eyes, then walk to the school's doors
in a quickly formed chain
(black, white, black, white),
holding hands and
singing, singing—we are young, we are spring-filled,
we are spirit-filled, we are eighth graders with the world
high above our heads; we are linked together and we
are laughing.

130

Squint

Claire Matway
First Place for High School Poetry, 2012

And it's Uncle Steve's house with the rough blue couches and bright lamps
and deer heads on the walls and sandwich materials
piled on the long low table in the kitchen;
it's three dogs and a view of wintry hills and red-lit radio towers;
Christmas Eve means
five cousins sprawled on the wooden floor amidst
crumpled wrapping paper and gift cards for T.J. Maxx,
a semicircle of aunts, uncles, grandparents
leaning in from folding chairs, cycling
by age through piles of gifts. Christmas Eve means
my uncle's best friend is standing by the tree, beer in hand,
gray stubble and plaid shirt and manly as ever
(and you will not know it by watching,
but he and my uncle are best friends in the sense that
they will never leave each other their whole lives,
that they are each other's
arms). They will not live together
because this is rural Pennsylvania and
they would just be fags.

My uncle's lover stands by the Christmas tree,
squinty-eyed and chuckling and then
he is next oldest in the age cycle of
gift-unwrapping (I am picking at the tag of
a magenta velour hoodie I will never wear)
and Mama hands him a calendar for the new year,
pictures of skylines planted in its gloss and
he is surprised and brandishing his beer and laughing and,
"Twenty years I've been coming to Christmas! This
is the first damn present I ever got!" And his squinty eyes
could almost be watery, but the room is too even or soft
with the rumble of my family talking and,
"First present I get in twenty freakin' years!" and
Christmas Eve means
my grandmother's on the couch laughing,
picking at a candy wrapper; I am
blinking at the wrong none of us ever saw and at
the plastic-wrapped square of cardboard and skylines
that forms a different story, tucked gently

under a plaid-clad arm. Christmas Eve means
the little pile of presents that forms by his chair the following year
and the sense of, "Yeah, you dumb or something? Those are yours!"

They Ask and They Judge

Iman Mazloum
First Place for College Poetry, 2014

Whenever they see me they ask,
Where are you from?
No. Really. You can't be just Canadian.
What's your ethnic background?

I respond with the long answer.
My mom is Indian but born in Uganda.
My dad is Lebanese.
So I am mixed and multi-culti.

That's so cool, they reply.
I know, I smile.
But the assumption is always there.
Oh, are you Pakistani?

But it's not as bad as France,
Where they say you are French, but if you are black. . . .
They ask, Which country are you from?
Then they classify you as "something else."

They want to discuss my culture with me.
Which is something I've learned to appreciate.
And if they are Pakistani,
They want to make a friend who reminds them of home.

But it's not as bad as India,
Where you are born into a caste.
They ask if you are an untouchable.
Then they judge your ability to be human.

Where are you really from?
China, I wish I could reply.
My parents tell me to say I'm from Timbuktu.
I'd rather talk about Tim Hortons doughnuts.

But it's not as bad as Russia,
Where they say you are all equal, but if you are a gypsy. . . .
They ask you if you are orphaned.
Then they ignore you until you disappear.

I've got it good.
They want to know out of curiosity.
They want to know why I speak English well,
But look olive-ish brown.

Our diversity should be celebrated,
Even if we might just want to be a proud national.
Because we are global citizens.
And only education will heal our skin-caused wounds.

Rural Vandalism

Michael Mingo
First Place for College Poetry, 2015

My hometown's demographic data
is a punch line: ninety-five percent white,

five percent black bear. The cedar trees
outnumber the residents seven-to-one.

The mountains are an empty set. According
 to my folks, they—the understood they—

will never move to our neck of the woods;
the jobs are in Paterson and Kearny.

"We moved out, and they moved in." It's easy
to feel secluded, on guard, as shadows

branch out over the roof. The other night someone
dropped a stone through our windshield.

The glass fragments gathered on the dashboard
will not reflect the culprit's face. We all,

I'm sure, have our knee-jerk suspicions.
The laws of probability say otherwise.

The Woman, the Paradigm

Deborah Monti
First Place for High School Poetry, 2014

Skin starts crinkling
As my arms start peeling and my hips start widening
And my freckles begin disintegrating as my face morphs
Into a soft-cheeked big-lipped paradigm
Of the Hispanic woman society has made me out to be.
Until my hair turns a jet-black shade
My eyes an almond brown and my skin a deep cocoa
I cannot speak Spanish
They see that I am pale and lanky and sheltered
And until I crack with Hispanic features
They will not believe my native tongue.
I too had a dream
But it was of sweet bonbons and the local radio station
The chain linked fences and cheap fireworks
Grandmother's sweet kisses.
With a tattooed back, a lip pierced, and a faint accent
I've signed my life to be a Latina teen from Queens
Well I might be
Because that's the only Hispanic woman portrayed on TV

College Kids

Leslie M. Mullins
Honorable Mention for College Poetry, 2001

We all went together
to the bar down the way
in the so-called hood.

We all passed the grown men
on the curb drinking 40 ounces
and playing craps.

We all saw the homeless woman
holding her two children
very close to her bosom.

We all saw the vacant lots,
which were filled with decaying trash
and broken glass.

We all felt the despair in the air
and saw it on the faces
of all the children.

But after the drinks and
the laughs we all went back
to our dorm rooms.

And when asked the next day
did we want to do community service. . . .
We all did nothing.

Keeping

Emily Nagin
First Place for High School Poetry, 2005

We are sitting on the jungle gym and it is cold and it makes the backs of my legs ache. Tobacco smoke curls messages in the sky, insubstantial and old, curvy as a jazz tune. The radio sings tinny into the air and the lyrics catch on the words scratched in the pole by my left shoe. Everything catches there, smoke circling it like a frame, my eyes snag on it and it makes a run in my pupil. Blow me Anne Frank. Two years ago I drank hot cocoa in the same house where she wished for sun and bicycles. Stood close enough to her bedroom walls to touch and tried hard to breathe. Our tour guide had a Dutch accent and a gap between her teeth. The people behind me spoke Yiddish and their words took me back to the yeshiva gym where I drank grape juice in a plastic cup. A boy with big ears blew the shofar and the rabbi spoke in Hebrew, which I didn't understand, and it was cold and my skirt stuck to my tights and I hated the kids who understood what he was saying and I hated their stupid skull caps and I hated being Jewish. On Ash Wednesday my school went to church and while the other girls knelt and opened their mouths for wafers, Alex the Atheist and I sat together and rubbed the ashes from our foreheads. I didn't know the prayers so I mouthed the blessing for wine and bread during the Hail Marys and understood why it is we hold onto things. In my head and in my heart and in my soul the radio sings thin tendrils into the sky and mixes with the smoke. I knew the video for this one. The singer is a dead bird.

Eye to Eye

Emily Nagin
First Place for High School Poetry, 2006

The sign says that 100 people
stood chest to back to shoulder
to cheek to neck to thigh to eye
to eye in each boxcar.
Inside it smells of old wood and old air,
the windowsills are worn smooth
by years of hands, brushing.
My two friends and I spin slow circles
and I try to imagine us,
wrist to wrist, together here.
She is Jewish. He is not,
but if anyone told, they'd take him too.
His chest is delicate as a bird's.
Her mouth is set and stubborn.
I think of us in camps together, their faces
going up in smoke and I want to hide them
somewhere safe, bulletproof.

I think that when age has carved canyons
through my cheeks I will still remember
this day. How we stood,
the hair on our arms rising,
the pressure in our throats.
I think I will remember the still air,
the smooth windowsills.
I think I will remember
her set mouth, his delicate ribs.
I think I will remember it perfectly.

Isn't Music the Universal Language?

Jéri Ogden
Honorable Mention for High School Poetry, 2004

You like who? Who's John Mayer? You know . . . solo artist . . . guitar player, I try to explain. Puzzled looks overtake their faces as we look through the CD racks. I pick up Vanessa Carlton and the *A Walk to Remember* soundtrack. They pick up some mainstream rapper who is on every music television station claiming to be "the next greatest rapper hip-hop has ever seen." Every popular radio station I switch to, I am sure to hear one of his four singles, which are actually all the same song just remixed and featuring some mainstream R&B singer.

That new 50 Cent album is the hotness! Excitement overtakes them now. Doesn't it seem wrong that he's only popular because he was shot nine times? *No. He's gangsta. More gangsta than John Mayer,* they tell me. I don't want to debate with these kids. They are friends of a friend so I don't say anything else.

Before we leave they buy the latest releases by 50 Cent and Jay-Z. *Why she act so white?* They whisper, thinking I'm not listening. I pretend I'm not, wonder to myself how someone can *act white*, and pay for my CD. The cashier looks a little like John Mayer. He winks at me when he hands me my change.

Coloring Paper

Shanquae Parker
Honorable Mention for High School Poetry, 2012

I thought I could slither my slender hands
across the black and white keys
and they would hear my pain,
trying to clear a path for hope with vibrations.
But no, their deaf ears didn't listen to me.
I prayed the night before, for a miracle,
for them to hear again.
But they didn't want to hear.
Because my hands weren't to their liking?
They were black,
my hands were black.
So when I sat at the piano and brushed my hands
against the black and white keys, they didn't hear me
and their blind eyes didn't want to see me.
So, I will stain my brittle black words
onto this white frigid sheet of paper,
and maybe they will feel me.
They will feel how cold and weak my heart is
when I write with my black hands.
And just maybe, one day when I get the courage,
they can see how I look when I read these words
that I colored on this here paper.

Give

Alexis Payne
Second Place for High School Poetry, 2014

My father's eyes become wide sometimes
when he cries

for his people and the lost years

language

the breathless beaten
stripped and whipped
men who look like him.

my father's eyes are brown like his skin
like his scarred hands that screw screws into

metal studs. the nail gun
pops and sputters.

why does my father cry?
as he begs me to take this world
and make something
more than his tools

as he stretches the tape measure
across the window frame and
adds in his head
as he pops the chalk box on the drywall
and cuts with his utility knife
perfect lines and angles

as he leaves for work every morning
at 5 a.m. with his eyes tired,
his knees pained
his back sore.
carpenter. proud.
he writes his name on everything
he owns. why does my father cry?
when the men at the site
think he's a laborer because
his skin is brown like his eyes.

he teaches me
to ensure trim on doorways
and lay hardwood floors.
he teaches me to be strong.
and proud.

he tells me that the world is mine

my father's eyes are brown like his skin
like his arms that reach around me and hug

like his tears that burn his cheeks
like sulfur or acid.
why does my father cry?

because his hands are all he has to give

not a language or a culture, but his hands
with their lines that I've memorized
like a poem

his hands

my father grits his teeth
and blinks.

pluck him out and in a different
time, my father would scream,
my father would kill.
he would smash glass and break wood

but here my father cries.
he cries
tears into his hands
and they run down the lines
like rivers.

Being Human

Alexis Payne
Second Place for High School Prose, 2015

Part One: Hair

Little dark girls with naps. Little dark girls with naps play on the street corner at midnight while little dark boys shoot craps in the hallway, whisper to each other about the politics of survival. Little dark girls with naps make sandwiches with bologna and twist hips on the sidewalk, tumble in heels too big for small feet. Little dark girls, little dark girls. . . .

You don't see me in magazines. Hair thick like a brillo pad, short mini fro like the way I came out of the womb womb womb. I lie. I was bald when my mother birthed me, my head like the shiny back of a new penny. What is hair anyway? You don't see me in magazines.

Sometimes you see girls with curls that run down their shoulders in ringlets, exploding from their heads in long, long tresses. Mixed Chicks product line, like being black is a crime of sorts, praising the girl whose hair feels like hair. Mine reminds you of wool you say. Some days I wish I had hair like yours. Some days I don't. These days I more often am grateful for me. Those days I wished everyday that I was you you you.

In elementary school, I thought there were more white people in the world. The Flats look like beer cans and Hillbillies and people who are broken and . . . have . . . no . . . class. What's that mean anyway? Have no class? We went swimming in a pool down the road from our school and I didn't wanna get my hair wet because it was straight and I loved it and it made me look like you you you. You were beautiful.

Little dark girls with naps.

This woman walks up to me and she says . . . *Is that all your hair really?* I say no. I should say yes. I should say . . . is that all *your* hair really? I should lean forward like she does, petting at my scalp like I am something to be gaped at. I don't say anything. Does that make me weak? *I used to do hair you know? I used to do hair but I never did hair like yours.* Yours. Yours. Little dark girl with naps. Her hand still rests there, trying to figure out the maze of braids that confuses her. She must solve the mystery that is me. I smile wide at her, tight-lipped. I am fake. I am weak. I don't say anything. . . . *Oh I see. I could tell. I could tell it wasn't real, I just wasn't so sure.* I pack up my things and she moves her hands. I am still smiling. Am I weak for this? For not knowing what to say? She doesn't know. She grins at me and shrugs. *Mhm. Mhm. Mhm.*

Hips and hair. Little dark girl with naps. Celebrated naps. Look at her hair. She's a proud black woman who don't need no man. Afrocentric! Making statements that bounce off societal expectations and stick to the places that burn the most.

I am not making a statement. I am not making a statement. I like naps. I like naps like the ones my grandmother had when she came out of the womb womb womb.

My hair is in curls too thick to see. I like weave sometimes. I like straight hair and big hair. I like hair. I like my hair. In so many shades of black, I am tumbling. I just want to float away, to be a human . . . human, human.

Part Two: Purpose

At a church retreat we discuss what the word "purpose" means to people of the world. I say that for a lot of people, purpose simply means to survive. My church doesn't understand that: "Maybe in West Africa, where people are fighting Ebola. But not here."

Not here. Not here. Like we are some grand and holy nation. Like we all have never been to prison, never felt hopeless, never had the lights shut off because we couldn't pay the bill.

I want to tell them of the boy who got shot on Saturday night. The boy who went to prom with us. The boy who graduated. He was 18. 18. 18. The news says that he died very matter-of-factly, dryly, like there's nothing particularly remarkable about a black boy getting shot in the head head head:

Mr. Turner had been found in the stairwell, shot in the head, and was taken to UPMC Presbyterian where he died Sunday.

He died Sunday. The Lord's Day. The holy day. We pick apples on Sunday. We sing songs about Jesus with a guitar, smile at the little boy who runs across the carpet in bare feet. Chandeliers dangle above our heads and we are warm. We sleep in this mansion in Ohio with room and rooms and rooms. A tree house and a lake sit out back with a dock for paddle boats, and a cute statue of a little white dog.

. . . he had been found in the stairwell, shot in the head.

What is your purpose in life when you've seen twenty of your friends shot in the head head head? What is your purpose in life when no one will give you a job because you had to sell drugs because you didn't know how to do anything else because public education never felt like teaching you how to read because politicians are rich people who can't see beyond their own noses . . . what what what. Your purpose is to survive. To pay bills. To find food. To take care of the people you love. It is not to change the world. Some people simply don't have that luxury.

When I go back home, I tell my best friend to be safe. I tell him not to go to places where he might die. That sounds ridiculous because he could die anywhere. He could die in the middle of a church. I don't understand why some lives mean more than others.

"He was a thug."

"He chose to live that life."

"The boy was asking for it."

"You hear they found weed in his back pocket?"

"You hear they found weed?"

My best friend tells me that he's going to get himself a gun: "It's crazy out here. That way nothing can happen to me." I want to tell him not to. But I don't want him to die. I don't say anything. Guns scare me. Scare me.

Maybe you haven't even begun to ask the right question:

"You hear he was a human being?"

. . . a human being . . . a human being. . . .

Grocery Shopping

Ben Pelhan
Third Place for College Poetry, 2006

If I were black
I wouldn't care that Dr. King
plagiarized whole pages
of his doctoral dissertation
for which he was awarded
his Ph.D. in theology.
Whole paragraphs!

But I'm white,
so I have to imagine him hunkered
down in a basement digging
through stacks of essays
with scissors
and glue
and a devious grin and
one of those made-for-TV
Mwahaha's, and a desk lamp casting
shadows across half his face.

Now imagine strawberries
sitting red and ripe in the fruit aisle
suddenly getting sour and jumping on the floor,
demanding to be treated like bananas.

Because I am white,
I have to ask that Boston
U. revoke Dr. King's Ph.D.
Since my grandparents hail from a place
called Scotland, I must request that we call
him Mr. King instead.

But consider
chocolate-covered strawberries.
What aisle do they belong in?
Fruit or candy? Or maybe
in the frozen foods aisle
because you have to keep them frozen
or the chocolate will melt.
Then they would just be strawberries.

Now since we all know
that without his Ph.D.,
Mr. King never could have led
the Civil Rights Movement, I have to ask
that we return to segregating schools, bathrooms,
and even water fountains. Don't you think

that at the state fair
they shouldn't always just give
out the blue ribbon to the biggest strawberry
or the yellowest banana? Maybe
they should judge on taste.

Speaking of taste,
did Hendrix ever win a Grammy?
I can't remember, I just keep hearing
those six strings with their upside down howl.
Oh don't get me started on left-handed
people. Maybe chocolate-

covered strawberries don't belong
in an aisle. Maybe we shouldn't
even have aisles and any fruit
can be whichever fruit it wants to be,
regardless of taste, color, or vine of origin.
But "that's anarchy," as my professor
would say. Did I mention he's
left-handed. He's also black,
but don't make everything about race.
Black is just all the colors combined. Dark
is the absence of light. White is the absence
of any color. White light
is the absence of imagination.
Imagination is the absence

of ignorance. But why do blue
ribbons have to be blue?
Lead Belly never won
a Grammy, but Jamaica

got its bobsled team,
and even though I'm white,
I think we should give
Mr. King an honorary
Ph.D. He's earned it.

Racism at School

Justin Platek
Third Place for High School Poetry, 2007

I. Entering: Outside

Intimidated white kids
walk fast down the crumbly
street to school,
staring at their blue-fade shoes
and sprinkles of tiny pebbles.
Clusters of black kids
line the street,
making their walk a parade,
bleating comments out of the sides of their mouths
and making threats with tight fists.
The white kids just walk,
bloody and bruised from verbal assaults
on their self-conscious skin.

II. Class

Erykah, Tonique and Desmond
are the only black kids in Mr. Price's
third period PSP English.
"Man, why we gotta be in the white class?"
Desmond says from their secluded corner
in the back of the classroom.
Other than the acidic words
they occasionally whisper loudly amongst themselves,
they are good kids, smart
with good grades and smiles to prove it.
Desmond runs on the varsity track team
instead of hustling weight on the dark streets;
Tonique sings in the Lighthouse Baptist Church's choir
instead of making babies like her sister Ronnie;
Erykah writes poetry after her mom uses coke at the dinner table
instead of taking some for herself;
the easy way out.

They are some of the best kids
in the room,
but all Mr. Price sees are three blacks

in an otherwise white class
that sit unattached to each other,
laugh out loud during lectures and
spill some slang onto their term papers.
Instead of getting to know who they are,
he hatefully describes them and their behaviors
as *monkeyish*
in the closed confines of his mind and
during the privacy of lunch in the teacher's lounge.
Some sniff and snicker,
but no one says a thing.

III. Gym

There is a red Mason–Dixon Line that slices
the slippery hardwood in half,
the white kids on the left, the black kids on the right.
The coaches don't set it up this way,
society does.
Charlie is the only one who dares
to cross the line, but he pays for it.
The other white people don't like him,
he is a wannabe and a traitor,
a snag on an expensive cream sweater.
They spit slurs on his face
and place sloppily handwritten threats
on wrinkled sheets in his locker.
Nobody on the right side of the line cares
as he crosses to play basketball or ping-pong
with them,
except for the small group
whose noses sit above the horizon,
and the one whose
arms stretch high, attached to closed fists
when Charlie walks by.

IV. Lunch

There are three multiethnic tables
in the cafeteria:

two are all female,
one has four people,
and none at all are cool.

V. Study Hall

Two teachers monitor the study hall
of fifty-seven tired students.
They glare at all the computer screens
keeping constant watch,
but paying long, close attention to the black kids',
expecting to see email accounts and music sites
instead of schoolwork.
They quickly encircle the room on their mission,
almost running,
their prim skirts rustle wrinkled
and their not-so-high heels make more noise
than anybody's mouth
as they trip over network cords
in their frantic frenzy
when the room erupts in laughter
in collective, uncolored amusement.

VI. Leaving: Outside

The clusters watch the parade
hesitantly march past,
fingers numb from the ignorant position of hands.
Violence is rare just outside,
but victims here are plentiful.
In fact,
there hasn't been a day
where everybody whose feet
rest upon the sidewalk
or whose rears sit against the cold
stone wall
has
survived.

The Diary of a Suspected Terrorist

Bani Randhawa
Third Place for High School Poetry, 2014

i am the seventeen years of removing the shoes from my feet,
the phone from my pocket,
the brown from my skin,
as I stand in airport security,
the red hot shame that fills my throat to a close as the
officer swabs my father's turban for explosives.

i am the pungent turmeric that stains the pots in my mother's kitchen,
its smell lingering in the wool of my sweaters and the strands of my hair.
i am the summation of all of the times i have stood and recited the pledge of allegiance
in school, hand over my heart, the taste of last night's aloo matar still lingering on
    my lips.

my mother places her rough hand over mine, aged from the hours spent
chopping onions for masala and massaging coconut oil into her thick black hair.
her servile eyes turn down, away from the bright blue ones that glare at her
"yes sir, you may pat me down," she whispers.
yes sir, to the man who hears her thick accent and pulls her aside.
yes sir, to the man who pulls open her empty pockets and shakes out her shoes.
yes sir. yes sir. yes sir.

i walk through the metal detector next to my mother, but not with her,
for she is the fourteen-hour plane rides that span the eight
thousand miles between her house and her true home,
the yellow ambassador cabs on the streets of Kolkata that honk away the hours of
    the night,
the muffled long-distance phone calls she makes that reduce
her voice to the faintest of whispers.

my father is defeated as he sits to retie his shoes.
perhaps it is his silent demeanor and blank eyes
that he has while being patted down that say more
than his empty answers to the officers.
i watch the triumph diminish from his tired eyes as
he questions the American flag on his lapel,
the hamburger in his belly, the
United States of America.

Co-Ed

Bridget Re
Second Place for High School Prose, 2014

Mud is splashed all over my teammates as they come off the field smiling. We have just won against one of our biggest rivals and are moving on to the next round of play-offs. With a shortness of breath, everyone talks about the great plays of the game, and how utterly exhausted they are. But all I can say is how tired my hand is from filling up water bottles for an hour. I am the only girl on our school's "co-ed" varsity soccer team. As I continue to commit my time and heart to this team, I become anxious waiting every game for my coach to call my name and tell me it's my time to play. But each time I find my hopes dashed as the buzzer goes off signaling the end of yet another game. Whenever I talk to my coach about soccer and the lack of time I get on the field, he tells me, "You're going to get a lot more playing time coming up soon."

Yet continuously I find myself on the bench with that empty promise ringing through my ears. Nonstop, I wonder why I never get played. Is it because I'm not good enough, even though my coach tells me that I'm "a huge asset to the team," or is it because I am a girl? My mind settles on the latter, and I feel even more ostracized by my "team."

I remember at the end of one game the two teams lined up to shake hands, and even though I had not played I stood in line too. I was used to getting odd looks during lineups like a rare breed of animal on display at a zoo. But this time as I walked through hearing the echo of "good game . . . good game," my ears perked up in surprise to hear one boy blurt out, "Oooh, hello cutie!"

My mind froze at first out of disbelief. Once my shock subsided, a snowball effect took place inside my head conjuring up ideas as to why he had said that. I was jolted out of my trance when I heard my friend behind me crack up laughing, and I decided to laugh to hide the discomfort I felt inside. However, feeling subjected to this stranger's lewd comment, I subconsciously crossed my arms over my chest and looked down at the ground, determined not to make eye contact with anyone. I felt ashamed. Who was I to think that I could actually play on an all-boys team?

After this incident, I became more aware that I was a girl encroaching on a male team. No longer could I pretend that I was acknowledged as just "one of the guys." All of a sudden, I became aware of the wandering, degrading stares I got as I bent down to stretch along with my teammates, which made me disgracefully take a place in the back of the line—hoping to go unnoticed. I became aware of the offensive sexual comments they made on the bus rides home from games, which made me yearn to become invisible. I became aware of what they said about me. I became aware that I was not played because I'm a girl.

Then the day came where I could no longer take it. After sitting on the bench during yet another game, I walked up to one of my best friends on the team and started to cry—a very girlish thing to do. Nonetheless, he listened as I vented to him about how I didn't feel I was good enough to play on the team, and in turn replied by telling me how much I gave to the team only to get nothing back. He kept on telling me over and over again that I should switch to field hockey because I would "get more out of being on an all-girls team."

"Great," I thought to myself. Even my best friend noticed that I was a fox in the hen house. I was used to these comments though it still hurt me that he wanted me gone as well. It wasn't the first time someone told me I should switch to an all-girls team instead of being with the boys. I think they believe I'm not capable of playing with boys twice my size. They also don't want to see a girl get hurt or knocked around. I used to be determined to show all of those people that I was going to stick with soccer and not give into sexism.

But discouraged from never being played, I stopped caring about something that was once a passion. The next year when fall sports came around, I begrudgingly decided to play field hockey, recognizing that prejudice had won.

In the words of Dr. Martin Luther King, Jr., "Whatever affects one directly, affects all indirectly. I can never be what I ought to be until you are what you ought to be. This is the interrelated structure of reality." Dr. King was trying to convey the idea that when you treat someone as an outsider, you end up promoting separation and prejudice. The lives of all people are entangled and influenced by each other. So injustice to an individual threatens justice for everybody. One might believe that any act of injustice that happens to someone else will not affect them, but in the long run, it does.

My story may be small on the scale of sexism; however, I regret my decision in switching because I now realize that I was only aiding the enemy. Due to my inability to speak up, I was unable to stop the prejudice that surrounded me. I was tempted by the easy way out, not realizing that I was aiding a bigger cause than just my lack of field time. For that I will always be remorseful.

77D

Duncan Richer
First Place for High School Poetry, 2006 (Tie)

It is so late,
it's actually early.
The solemn glow of the streetlight reflects off the wet dew
glinting observantly on the pavement.

The bus moans—
it turns 6 today.
Nobody is celebrating because busses can't eat cakes.

I sit there, quietly
B
    U
        M
           P
        I
    N
G
on the seats with cushioning like carpet
at the federal building where my aunt works.
B
    U
        M
           P
        I
    N
G
All the white men with business suits and Rogaine-smeared scalps
are also
B
    U
        M
           P
        I
    N
G
And so are the loud black girls with Wendy's uniforms
and no-cream coffee as dark as they are.
They are

B
      U
           M
                 P
           I
      N
G
too.
The strong bus driver is
bumping.
But that's because he has his seat belt on real tight.

And when the bus
B
      U
           M
    P
S
real hard because the city is poor and potholes are invading
and the black girl's coffee

makes the white man's shirt brown,

everybody just sits patiently. They become bystanders.
They become witnesses. They become spectators.
They know he's going to explode.

And when he does,
everybody acts like they just saw the chick
flick with the predictable ending.

And then they
step
    off
the bus's stairs and I try not to notice the crying girl
with not enough napkins.

The American Boss

Rachel Rothenberg
First Place for High School Prose, 2010

You think to yourself, I don't know anyone like that. You tell these kinds of stories as if they were the hypothetical things that happen to other people, things said by other people, people who don't live where you are. Those kinds of people live in the South, in the suburbs, in the red states. You don't live in the South, you don't live in a red state, and, by God, you don't live in the suburbs. So you're safe, you're off the hook. You have already attained enlightenment.

Right?

Here is what happened to me.

My parents had these friends, the Ms, a married couple with two children who lived a couple of blocks away. They were South Africans, white, and used to complain how white South Africans were always portrayed badly in movies, like Russian gangsters and overeducated British men. Mrs. M was a small woman with flyaway curly hair and cheeks that turned red whenever she laughed, which was often. She had voted for the African National Conference (ANC), much to her Afrikaner in-laws' horror, and wore an apron printed with the face of Nelson Mandela.

But this story is not about Mrs. M, or about her husband, whose family had hated Mandela so much. This is about Mr. M's boss, the American one, the one who wore the Obama pin on his lapel the night we had dinner. This is about the boss' wife, who held charity events for the underprivileged.

Like I said, it could be anyone.

My father went to San Francisco on business, and Mrs. M, perhaps sensing my mother's loneliness, called and asked us over to dinner.

"The old man's boss is coming," she said, "and his wife. They're awful old people, but we'll have some wine and make the best of it." She sounded desperate, so Mom and I put on our Sunday best and went over.

The American boss was tall and lean, with bright sparkling blue eyes. He looked like a Kennedy, all angles and jawline. He shook my hand vigorously. His wife was small and slim, in a tailored jacket and a well-fitted skirt. They looked like any other professional couple, the kind who represent the progressive establishment of America, the ones who are supposed to lead the way in changing the world.

We had dinner: roast lamb and rice and baked fennel. In time, the conversation turned to my mother's job: a Presbyterian minister, she worked as a student pastor at a church in Homewood. At hearing this name "Homewood," the boss' wife wrinkled her nose slightly. It was barely perceptible, just a quick up and down, but it was there all the same. In situations like these, I am usually shy and quiet, so I have become an expert in observing. I looked down at my plate, the lamb looking dry and greasy against the white.

The Ms' children went to the local elementary school. The boss' children were homeschooled.

"Though," the boss' wife said, "we haven't always done that." She laughed and tossed her hair. "We aren't one of those crazy Christian families!"

"Ah," said Mrs. M, a tight smile on her face. Next to me, my mother's nostrils flared. She smelled blood.

"Where did your children go before you homeschooled them?" she asked.

"Oh, Homewood Montessori. But we left because we didn't think it was a very good environment for the children." She added a deep emphasis on the word *environment* as if we knew exactly what she meant.

Except Mr. M, who still struggled with English from time to time, raised his head up and said, "I'm sorry—what environment?"

"Oh, well, you know," said the wife, "some of those kids—well, the father up and left, went to God knows where, and the mother's never around, since she's working. They're home by themselves. And they're eating processed foods, too. They were giving our kids sugar cereals there. I mean, I'm telling you," she said, "they need a stable household. They need to be civilized."

Mom dropped her knife. "Excuse me," she said, in a tight, hard voice, and ducked to pick it up.

"I'll tell you what the problem is," said the boss. "The problem is this busing they had in the Seventies. It was better when everyone could just go to a neighborhood school with . . . well, with people like them. Don't you think?" he asked my mother.

She said nothing. I looked from Mom to the Ms to the boss' wife and back again, all the time wondering, *Did they just hear what I heard? Did he seriously just argue in favor of what I think he argued in favor of?* But they were only silent, and so was I.

The rest of the night, whenever I looked at them, I felt a hot constriction in my chest, as if something were about to burst. The conversation turned to the upcoming election, and the boss and his wife proudly told us they were going to support Obama. "Such an educated black man," the wife said.

Not long after, we got up to leave. As I walked out the door, Mrs. M came up to me. She had been washing dishes, wearing the Nelson Mandela apron. She caught my hand and squeezed it hard, then let me go.

In the car, Mom was silent. I turned the radio up as far as it would go. We turned onto the asphalt darkness of our street, the streetlights illuminating the just-paved blacktop. We pulled into the garage and sat there a while. I could almost hear Mom thinking.

Finally she said, "Rachel, I taught you a horrible lesson tonight."

"What's that?" I asked.

She sighed and ran both hands through her hair. "If you learn one thing from me, it should be this: when things like this happen to you, don't ever be silent."

In retelling this story to people, I am always met with looks of incredulity. "Did they really say that?" they ask. "And they're from the East End? And he was wearing an Obama pin?"

But the fact remains that something that pervasive doesn't come from living with Republicans or living in the South or even from living in the suburbs. It's born within, somewhere in the most animal parts of the brain where humans learn to hate other humans, to covet material goods and privilege and anything that allows someone to prosper on the back of someone else, and cover it up with a thin veneer of respectability. And, as in all things, only a loud noise, a sudden shock, a lightning bolt of truth, can bring it out of hiding. But it's hard to handle a lightning bolt. I didn't say anything that night because I was afraid. Fear is what drives every negative human impact. And, as we move into this bold new future of ours, we must learn to be unafraid.

I drove through Homewood a few days later with my mother and a few women from the church. They were talking and laughing and swapping stories. I sat in the back and listened for the hum of change. It was there, I think, barely perceptible but alive. And I leaned back and thought about how much you could miss if you didn't listen, didn't observe. Almost a whole world.

Segregation

Frances Ruiz
Honorable Mention for College Poetry, 2005

I have a dream that my four children will one day live in a nation where they will not be judged by the color of their skin but by the content of their character.
—Dr. Martin Luther King, Jr.

Waaaaaaaaaaaaasssssup my niggah!
the drunk brown man
beside me in Chief's says
as he slaps the back
of a dark black man.
You have to be careful
when you say stuff like that,
the dark black man says,
I mean, with your complexion
and all. A quick downing
of a shot, the blond female
bartender wipes a glass.
You ain't black enough to
be called my niggah,
you ain't black enough to
be called my niggah, I sez,
you ain't black enough.

Freshman year, orientation,
"minorities" in a newly carpeted
room. "We, as people of color,"
the director begins. Then
she pauses, looks at me,
her eyebrows raise, her eyes ask
what kind of a minority are you?
"We, as people of color, must come
together to support one another."
Her gaze falls on me again. We,
as people of color, C-O-L-O-R,
color. Not you, no, you're too white to
be cubana, too white to know how
to dance salsa, too white unless,
of course, your first language
is Spanish and you grew up

barefoot, picking
grapes with Mexican
migrant workers.

The Definition of Who I Am

Adam Saad
First Place for High School Prose, 2008

In the past few years, the threat of terrorism has gone through many color changes. As terror rose, so did fear. America identifies Arab with terrorism. In many forms of popular media, such as movies and television shows, Arab people or people who slightly resemble Arab people are stereotypically represented as "terrorists," "Al Qaeda," or "Ahmed." These portrayals of Arab people have them represented as either antagonists or as a source of comedy. Even I found humor in many of the common stereotypes of Arab people. With my friends, I would jokingly talk in the stereotypical voice of an Arab person, complete with bad grammar, misused words, and a heavy accent. My friends would laugh and I would laugh along with them. However, the reality of what these seemingly innocuous stereotypes can do is something that I am more than familiar with.

I am half-Egyptian and half-Chinese. My Chinese relatives live in New York, and I used to visit them quite often. However, after 9/11 my father decided that we would no longer travel to New York. When I asked him why, he simply stated that he was afraid of what people might do to us if they found out that we were Middle Eastern, afraid of people that did not know us and would simply pick out our last name and identify us as terrorists. We have not been to New York since.

Even in Pittsburgh, where we have lived for the past thirteen years, my father avoids bringing attention to his Middle Eastern origins. He has adopted the pseudonym of "Sam," which he derived from his Egyptian name "Essam," and further descending into his false persona, he claims that he is from Greece. This is not a joke. This is the story of a man who left his country to immigrate to America, and now he does not tell people his real name or what country he is actually from. One day a young girl asked me if I had any family in Greece. I had no response. I was completely unprepared for this question because I had never given my father's alter ego any real consideration. I was faced with a moral dilemma: whether I should lie and disavow my heritage or whether I should tell the truth and destroy the image that my dad had built up in our community. I chose to lie. I talked about how I had a family there and how they grew olives, none of which was true. Afterwards, I reflected on what I had just done and what it must feel like for my father to keep up this charade every day. I thought of all of the jokes that I had made about Arabs, and how they no longer seemed funny. It all came down to a question of identity and how I defined myself.

Am I Greek or Arab? I thought about this for a long time and tried to identify what I was. While pondering this question I was engaged in conversation with a man who coincidentally asked me where I was from, guessing that I was Puerto Rican. Still troubled in conflict, I answered that I was Chinese, again supplementing my actual ethnicity with a more commonplace ethnicity. I do not normally see myself as Chinese because, for the past six years, I have had few conversations with my

Chinese relatives. Since I had stopped visiting New York, my primary identity of myself was Arab, until now. If I tell people that I am Greek, then their perception of me is that I am Greek. This does not make me Greek, but to everyone else, that is what I am. Is my identity based on how I see myself or how other people see me? To many of the people in my community, I am Greek. To my friends, family, and myself, I am Arab.

I found that the definition of myself must be defined by me and that the opinions of others are irrelevant. Let them come with their slurs, their jokes, and their insults. I do not feel anger towards them, only pity. I am Arab, and I neither fear nor care about what repercussions this may have. My jokes towards Arab people now have new meaning. Rather than finding them to be funny, I now find them to be a mockery of what it means to be an Arab person and of the difficulties that many Arab people must endure. It is my opinion that the bias that many people feel towards people of Middle Eastern origins is only a response reaction towards what people have perceived from The War on Terror, the terrorist villains in movies, and the comical Arab foreigners. I hope that people will move past this and become more understanding. More understanding of what it means to be equal. I quote Abraham Lincoln's first inaugural address, "We are not enemies, but friends. We must not be enemies. Though passion may have strained, it must not break our bonds of affection."

I feel that this is true and that we, as a society, should have learned from the one hundred plus years it has been since Lincoln gave this speech. No one should ever have to pretend that they are someone else or change their name because of where they come from, and this applies to all people, regardless of their ethnic background.

Behind These Eyes

Ari Schuman
Runner-up for High School Prose, 2010

1. Jerusalem, Israel.

"This is my rifle. There are many like it, but this one is mine."

Tan boys and girls laugh with rifle butts sticking out of the unsure space between their arm and torso. My ever-learned sister reassures me that it's normal here: everyone carries a gun when they're on leave—it protects them. I wonder within the temple of my mind just how ubiquitous hatred and suspicion must be for there to be polished Kalashnikovs in every 18-21-year-old's armpit.

I imagine lines of tan Israeli boys and girls, good Jewish citizens, being handed guns. The shaky ones are simply told, "This is normal," and the sure ones grit their teeth and stamp their feet, ready to fight. After hours of drilled reassurance, the shaky ones grit their teeth and stamp their feet along with the herd, ready to fight.

The animosity as the servicemen walk by an Arab stand or a grinning Yemeni man (leading his donkey and offering rides) is palpable. Every shot over the border strengthens it. Every rifle butt in an eighteen-year-old's armpit gives it fresh life.

2. Just Outside the Arab Quarter, Old City.

A small Arab boy pops up from behind an ancient, decrepit truck, a truck that screams sky blue with clouds of rust. I see his teeth.

"Hey! American!" he yells in his high-pitched, Arabic accent.

I turn, thinking my track jacket singles me out from among my family of Americans, and see more than the glimpse I barely caught. Bang. Crack. He's hitting the side of the truck, trying to get our attention.

"Yeah! You! American!" comes from somewhere, in the same high-pitched Arabic accent.

I shake off the yells. I think, in my quiet prejudice, that he is just trying to get me to buy some hawked goods just like the boy in all the movies. I think, in my quiet prejudice, "Thank God for rifles on leave." The next ancient archway couldn't pass over me quickly enough; the animosity had embraced me.

3. Arab Quarter, Old City.

The streets here are strewn with rubbish. The cobblestone roads of this old bazaar reek like the breath of a camel—pungent and acrid, the stench forces me to recoil. I do a little dance to avoid stepping in shit. I avoid the center of the road.

Indentations run through the middle of these ancient streets. The standing water, full of unimaginable bacteria, draws my eye. It's dark and dirty and I almost want to call it disgusting, but I can't bring myself to do that—even in the temple of my mind. To many of the wandering tourists here, the water is a microcosm of the Arab quarter.

Shrieks, yells, cries come from corners and catacombs. They all yell as one in a

Babel of languages, "For sale!" Open recesses with blinding fluorescent lights guide tourists in and out of religion. Men compromise themselves for thirty shekels in a place where, on principle, city sanitation is not expected. A scant few Americans venture into the places with scattered light and original wares, and they are simply resented while Yemeni and Saudi visitors are welcomed with open arms.

My brother and I dive into these corners and are pulled back by the scruffs of our necks, being warned of the danger. We don't see why we can't walk the winding streets which are only lit by occasional beams of sunlight. We don't see that our clear markers of Americana single us out and turn the society against us. In our naïveté, our guide says (reiterated later by our mother) that we could have been killed—don't we know what's going on in Gaza?

4. East Jerusalem, Jerusalem (where the New City keeps its lowest caste).

East Jerusalem was once separated from the west by a wall; where it stood, there is a neighborhood called the Seam. The Seam now stands as a gentrified neighborhood full of shopping carts and condos and mistreated men in keffiyehs. Women wearing burqas are sanctioned to the land of the Qur'an.

A sanctioned boy walked past our van; I assumed he was on his way to school. I saw it as a chance to say, "They're just like we are," with one thousand words. I swung up the lens, shooting through a tinted mirror, and, as the click sprung from our van, the boy turned, staring into the lens.

Click.

Our Israeli tour guide turned around; everyone seemed to be silently staring with the sides of their eyes. "It's best not to take pictures here," he said, voice low and guiding through the rearview mirror. I put the camera down, a little ashamed.

Through my shame, the penury of the city around me shone through. I watched Arab boys and girls walk by, and, in the temple of my mind I wondered if they were going to a school where they could do nothing but recite the Qur'an. In the temple of my mind I indulged the paranoia of talking heads. I saw their ragtag clothes and barely covered feet and I guarded my wallet (still inside the van). I passed the thin line between careful and prejudice. The animosity embraced me.

5. Western Wall, Jerusalem.

The devout men here pray by a section of wall where only men are allowed. We less-observant chosen ones look to them and feel guilty, just as they might like. They daven and they mutter, whispering incantations and arcane hymns of David to the Lord. Rain drips down from the tips of His fingers, hitting the paper yarmulkes of those less devoted. As I go to the wall, as I touch it, I feel nothing. No great revelation from above comes down to strike me like a bolt of lightning. I simply feel guilty.

I do, however, look over to my right. I see the women's section, considerably smaller and made for the same number of people, and my sister and mother crammed in among covered heads and long sleeves, standing out in their comparatively garish stripes.

Here, the ultra-Orthodox stand a foot taller than all others so that they may better look down upon us.

6. Near Haifa.

As I take a barely working elevator to my great-aunt's apartment, I can recall no memories of her. I know that she was my Grandmother's sister, and that she also survived the Holocaust, but I also know she wasn't in the camps—rather, she lived in Budapest. I don't know which floor to go to. The lights are out at every stop. As the halting contraption finally brings me to the right level, I leave, and there my family stands, waiting for the bags.

The apartment door opens as we approach. A wrinkled woman, wizened by age and experience, stands in the doorway, waiting. She is the only member of my family who would let us hug her that day.

Her Orthodox daughter and granddaughter come to talk and then lunch with us. The daughter would shake hands, and my father was surprised—the last time they met, she turned down his tacit invitation. However, the granddaughter remained pure, untouched by other men. She checked out of conversation, not willing to speak on topics outside of her box. As she left, she looked down at my hand; nothing was said, and nothing was done—what had happened was tacitly understood.

Here, the ultra-Orthodox stand a foot taller than all others so that they may better look down upon us.

7. Pittsburgh, Pennsylvania, now.

As I reflect upon these moments and memories, I see only prejudice. Be it my own, that of those in my own family, that of distant relatives, or that which caused a war, Dr. King would not have condoned a single action taken herein. Racism and prejudice is not limited only to America, and it not only done by those who do not write essays about racism. It is ubiquitous, omnipresent, invisible. Behind these eyes, in the temple of my mind, lies prejudice that does not want to come out, and, if it does, be it in war, in a bazaar, in a simple handshake, it is still prejudice that Dr. King would have fought vehemently against with every iota of his strength.

166

Breaking the Color Barrier

Themba Searles
Honorable Mention for High School Prose, 2010

Many expectations come with being black in America today, like the stereotypes that have been enforced since African people were enslaved in this country. Stereotypes play a large part in the psyche of American society; whether you are black, white, Latino, or Asian, there is an image that you are expected to encompass and live up to. In my life, this simple fact has had two sides to it—it seems as if living up to these stereotypes is just as condemning as rebelling against them, and my life has been a clear example of this truth.

Being raised in a black household had an indisputable effect on my personality as I grew up; with my older brother as a role model, I grew up absorbing what was African American culture. With my brother and his African American friends' influence, I grew up listening to, dressing, and speaking like an African American was expected to in America—not because I felt like it was who I was, but because I felt it was what I needed to do because of what I was. I was force-fed the latest fashions, the newest and most popular music, and taught that to be cool, one must "act black." This part of me was fiercely combated by where I was raised: a primarily white community and the school I attended, where the majority was white as well.

I would attend school everyday being one of the three African American students in my class, and I would live up to being one of the lone black students. I aimed to be the one to show off the urban music I listened to, or the latest fad in clothing to all of my white friends who didn't quite understand. I would go out of my way to flaunt the slang I was taught by my African American friends from outside of school. It was only midway through middle school when I took the time to contemplate why I spoke the way I did, the influence of the music I listened to, and why I wore jeans two sizes too large and shirts that hung low to my knees. This was the crucial turning point in my life when I decided that I didn't want to be the stereotype that those around me expected me to be, that I would take this moment of realization to change and decide for myself who I wanted to be.

From those I knew well, this break from the stereotype set by society was well-received, but from black friends of mine, there was a definite and immediate alienation. By not "acting black," it was accepted that I was "acting white," and therefore was not cool. Unfortunately, these relationships were unable to be revived.

Stereotypes are obviously present in America, and stereotypes lead to racism. In my break from black urban culture, I felt as if disassociating myself from the stereotypes of black people relieved me from the racism that went with it. My friends stopped viewing me as their black friend and began to see me only as their friend. But where this new persona of mine helped me to identify with those whom I really wanted to identify myself with, it estranged me from all else. Upon meeting people for the first time, they would see my skin color and be surprised by my refined speech. They would ask me why I spoke so well or be confused by the music I enjoyed listening to. These questions of my character were as piercing to me as any racist comment, as it was blatant racism. By acting black, all I was doing was enforcing an age-old stereotype and prolonging racist thoughts toward African Americans, and by not acting black I was met with disapproval and dirty looks. Black people I would meet would take one look at me, see that I was different, and think less of me for it. It took me quite a while to accept who I am and not become offended by either side, what they saw me as and what was expected from me.

In my indistinctness in deciding what race's characteristics I would most like to possess, I began to disassociate myself from my race, to be whatever I wanted to be without the burden of my skin color deciding who I was. The people I surrounded myself with embraced my racial independence, and I felt like stereotypes and racism were things that could never affect me again, until I was shocked back into reality.

My father had told me many stories about instances of racism against him and the disadvantages that his race brought with it when he was a child, but I had never encountered such circumstances until one day in the summer before my junior year of high school. I was walking to a free concert in the park with a friend of mine to see a local hip-hop artist one afternoon when a police car passed us on the street. My friend and I began to joke about how the police car was actually after me, as I was black and my friend was white. To our surprise, the squad car turned around and stopped in front of us in the street. My emotions could only be characterized as stunned with fear as I heard two white police officers ask us if they "could talk to us for a minute." Scared and confused, my friend and I slowly asked what the reason was and how we were involved. They asked us to walk into the street and place our hands on the trunk of the squad car. As I sheepishly walked over to the police vehicle, I began to put my hands in my pockets and was met with the screams of the male officer to, "Get your hands away from your pockets!"

I was scared and humiliated as they began to search my body for weapons of any sort, and the only sounds I could utter were the words, "Sir, what happened? What did we do?" After being ignored three or four times, we were informed that there had been a shooting at the park earlier and that we "fit the description."

I was dumbfounded; I never believed that in my lifetime I would hear words as terrifying as those. I was reminded of TV shows, movies, and stories where young black men would be arrested or wrongfully murdered for only the crime of fitting a description. I was a young black man in a residential area, dressed in a pair of blue jeans and a lacrosse camp T-shirt; I didn't realize I was so threatening. I was scared, I was offended, I thought of my mother who came to America from apartheid South Africa; I thought of my father who was raised on the south side of Chicago. I wondered what they would do in my situation, but I felt helpless; in that moment I thought of the Civil Rights Movement, of Martin Luther King, Malcolm X, and the Black Panther Party. I thought of horror stories of racist police officers shooting down young black men only for the reason of being black. As the officer ran his hands up the inside and outside of my pant legs, my arms, chest, and waistband, I saw a crowd begin to form, and three more squad cars arrived as backup. It was my first major run-in with the law and indisputably the most embarrassing moment of my life.

After interrogating us, I was able to breathe again—they released us because they were convinced that we actually were not the culprits in shooting at Mellon Park. In my quest for enlightenment in the field of stereotypes and race relations in America, this was a groundbreaking moment. After this warm summer afternoon, it was substantiated in my mind that racism still existed in America and that it was a major problem. It cast a shadow on my opinions of racism and stereotypes and my attempts to beat them. It dawned on me that the way that I saw myself was not nearly as important as the way that people perceived me. Racism is clearly still around and is cemented in my mind by the fact that eight policemen had to stop two young boys only because one was young and black. Incredible steps have been taken towards the end of racism, but although integration has already become part of our society, eliminating racial stereotypes is the next big step towards social equality, and that's monumentally more difficult.

Tobacco and Curry Leaves

Indhu Sekar
Second Place for College Poetry, 2001

I am from the West Virginian hills
but I have traveled to hot wastelands
where the cracked, brown earth thirsts for water.
I have traveled to hard cathedrals where the gray, cold stones
never feel the sun's golden warmth.
And I have traveled to humid coastlines
where the deep blue stretches to the white horizon.

I have seen the Malaysian hospital
where my mother was born,
its pink plastered walls now crumbled,
its wooden steps in splinters.
Heat has cracked the once-solid windows.

I have run through the streets where my father was a boy.
Inhaling Indian dust, feeling my skin
blacken under the sun, headily placing my feet
on brown soil, where my father once stepped.

I am a hillbilly. I am a Brahmin.
I have worn straw hats and cowboy boots
while my friends rubbed sweet tobacco.
I have lounged on porches playing guitar
while the paint peeled off jalopies sputtering by.

I have sat in church among women in gingham dresses
and men in blue overalls singing praises.
I have adorned saris and bindis in ancient Hindu
temples while the Ganges River hummed by.

I am West and East; I live among pickup trucks
and bull carts, breathe rhododendron and jasmine,
eat pizza and curry and seek the shelter
of all my homes.

My Mother Speaks

Ashley Smith
Second Place for High School Poetry, 2004

Two beautiful colours combined
are said to make another beautiful colour.
Red and blue make purple,
yellow and blue make green.
My skin was dark.
Being dark in Trinidad
was a symbol of beauty.
As the hot, tropical sun beat over my head,
I was not teased nor was I being insulted.
"What a beautiful personality your skin texture shows,"
my mother always said.
My brother was as dark as me.
With our wild-long nappy hair,
skinny legs, and knobby knees,
we would have forever
lost the confidence of being beautiful.
Our mother and father were set to leave us
for a place that we did not understand.
America.
My brother and I left a year after.
Leaving our six brothers and sisters,
our culture of Trinidad and Tobago
was lost only for a short-long while.
When we arrived,
the city of New York brightened above our heads.
It was cold.
From the first time I've seen it,
I've hated it.
Snow.
My skin tone dropped.
I was no longer the dark Trinidadian girl that I knew to be.
I was almost as white as the snow.
A pale Trinidadian complexion,
that was not a sign of beauty.
I loved New York, though;
it had so much multiplicity of people,
until we moved to Pittsburgh, Pennsylvania.
A place where our culture was nonexistent.
A place where our own people

were just as illiterate as the white people.
I hated school so much.
My brother and I went to separate schools.
I remember my brother got into a fight.
He said somebody called him a black African nigger.
Our accents were very strong.
We would get remarks such as,
"Are you from Jamaica," or
"How you get here? Did you come off a slave ship from Africa?"
The bad part about it was that the blacks
were saying it along with the whites.
I went home crying.
I told my mom what I wanted to be when I grow up.
I told her I wanted to teach Americans the word colour.
My mother looked at me and said,
"Child, if want to teach these Americans colour,
you have to learn how to spell colour first."
My mother was right.
Here in America colour was spelled c-o-l-o-r.
My brother and I spelled colour c-o-l-o-u-r.
I've realized that I would not be able to teach Americans colour.
They wouldn't understand,
nor would they want to learn.
My mother had her ninth and final child.
Oh how beautiful my baby sister was.
With skin that read beauty,
with skin of poetry that spoke of beauty.
She was never teased through life about herself,
only embarrassed that her parents were Trinidadians
and not Americans.
My sister did not understand.
She was being brainwashed by these children
who did not respect our culture
or what we are.
I sat down and told her,
"What we are, true people,
what we are, true colour."
My accent began to fade.
My brother and I began to talk like these Americans.

We finally became accepted.
Not really for what we are,
but now for what they've been hearing coming out of our mouths.
"You sound like us now.
You don't sound like them filthy Africans anymore."
My brother became a U.S. citizen.
I never did.
It's already bad enough I live in an illiterate country,
why represent them?
I stayed who I truly was,
a Trinidadian.
The people, who I call my friends,
still did not understand.
I still had insulting comments
which stayed underneath their tongues.
"Do you practice voodoo" or
"Does your whole family practice voodoo?"
I was smart—
being fifteen years old at the time, I did not care anymore.
I remember one of my friends asked me,
"I guess you know how to spell color right, huh?"
I smiled and said,
"Yes I do, c–o–l–o–u–r."
And I watched as I saw my friends sulk.
No American can teach me beauty,
because they don't know how to spell
my colour right.

Reading

Sarah Smith
First Place for College Poetry, 2005 (Tie)

Somebody wrote a poem, and they put Hitler in jail.
Somebody wrote a poem about the skin lamps, the ears floating in wineglasses.
Somebody wrote a poem so good they put it in the newspaper—
in the newspaper!
Somebody wrote a poem so the children did not have to die anymore.
It is a poem they will use as shoes. If they added hot water, it could be soup.
Somebody else wrote this poem, I don't have to.

Somebody wrote a poem about the way we ride the bus together,
how all the white college kids get on at the same stop.
I think somebody is watching me.

Somebody, ask Bill Clinton to write a poem with his saxophone and Ray-Bans!
Bill Clinton, tell us about Harlem. Tell us about the barefoot South.
I demand to see your bootstraps.
Nobody had to ask John Ashcroft to write a poem,
and he wrote a sonnet!
When does your biography come out?

Somebody wrote a poem for all the soldiers to read. Somebody wrote a poem
for the boy I went to high school with who burned Richard Wright's books.
That poem is about the boy's salty blood and crew cut.

Somebody wrote a poem, and it knows what I really thought about O. J.,
but I can't let you see it. This poem is as big and tall as me, but its eyes are not as blue.

Nobody wants these poems. They are too damn much trouble.
The libraries are webbed with blood. Nobody reads those poems if they can help it.

I saw the poem that they put up in Queens, it was as big as the 7 train
and every other moment the lights leapt out, and back on again,
and it was August for a little while longer, but everybody felt safe
reading in the dark.

Unmovable

Casey Spindler
Third Place for College Poetry, 2004

Me and my little cousin, Desmond,
stand in the black circle burnt
into his lawn late last night.

The aboveground swimming pool,
drained and burned,
now a ring of ash
and melted plastic.

I came over from my trailer
at the other end
of the park, past rows
of Confederate bumper stickers
and beer cases of empties.
I saw his mother at the window
dangling a joint from her lips.

When Desmond was old
enough to swim, she led
him to the creek.
A white boy ran to the rocks.
"Nigger water."
Next day, she bought
the pool with money
she didn't have.

Every day, after school
he'd float for hours—
his own private island.

Today, Desmond looks stronger
than anyone else in this park.
He stands where his ocean
used to be.
Stone-faced.

some assembly required

Javier Spivey
Third Place for College Poetry, 2017

my Abuela's spanish is quiet but loud with intention
it has that perfect comprehension of life with that wariness of death
and it's thick with the breath of viejo san juan down its neck
best believe it kept my mother in check
cuz Mamí's spanish is the creation of the new nuyorican nation
the 1970's formation sung by boleros on each station
tainos knew no lions until these women roared
heard from los calles de cupey to lex and 103rd

my spanish requires assembly
palabra puzzle pieces thwarted by toddler teeth marks on their corners
can't fit when they've been constantly chewed by caucasian mispronunciations
of my name culture and persuasion

ms. ellis in the pre-k
roll call on the first day
ja-vee-air or ha-vee-ay
too shy to speak up
Javier that's my name
anglicized by twenty-six-year-old ellis and her disciples
tyrannical tykes with whitewashed picture books as their bibles
jack was adventurous, phillip was charming
but in '01 at 8:05 a.m. my name was too alarming

syllables were stock to exchange in the morning
monikers meant cash for little white boys only
no bit-sized buyers wanted ha-vee or ha-vee-air, too many too exotic
but i woulda gone broke to be a max, tom, or dick

so Abuela and Mamí, i never intended to lose who i was
but i was sick of no one understanding:
perdona me, jota's like an h, this ain't no french
cuz i just wanted to uphold the hold on our third generation of american education
and the missing puzzle piece seemed to be assimilation

MIRA, when my accent faded and i waded out of spanglish shallows into the
hallowed river of gentrification, leading to the mouth of the melting pot flowing
into the ocean birthing our nation, i realized rita moreno lied. ain't no small fee to
be free in america. there's been a cost that can't be paid by any ancestor's loss, a cost

mi gente sees every time we turn on the tv and are reminded that the only way to make the great america what it used to be is to take any foreign flavoring out of its rice and beans y Mamí y Abuela i know you know that this man ain't the first to tell us we have to go. it's not just six-year-old toms and aged politicians building the partitions between nations and our coexisting visions, so what do i do when my *broken* spanish is the last of my ammunition?

permiso

con pacienca y fe help me put it back together
for once i realize our pride, i'll know no oppressor

One Shade Too Many

Kristen Swanson
First Place for College Poetry, 2013

To all the girls who ever judged me

Brown, brown, brown,
why are they always trying to pull me
down, down down?

Spanish girls thought because we all had brown
eyes, that we share Latina pride.
My father left when I was almost two.
Maybe he went back to Mexico—
nobody knew. They thought I
was trying to act tough and bold
because I was Mexican like them.

They thought because we all had brown
hair that looked black when the light
hit just right, that the root of our hair
was longer than the square root
of any number created out of thin air.
We were sistas, homies, tighter
than the braids gripping their scalps—
immigrant children, bilingual beauties.

They thought because we all had brown skin—
they said calling it that is almost a sin; "We
aren't brown, girl—we're tan,"
we're the caramel light mocha that melts
in your mouth; the sun-kissed chicas
all the boys dream about; a tan that
never fades—we don't need the sun
to make our complexion a perfection.

Brown, brown, brown,
why are they always trying to pull me
down, down down?

White girls thought because we all had brown
eyes that I grew up in the same suburban
neighborhood. They thought
I was Italian and that it was ironic

I hated pasta—I thought their attitudes
smelled like sour garlic bread.
My mom had speckled freckles around
her light green eyes—they assumed all my brown,
brown genes came from my dad's side.
They thought because we all had brown
hair, wavy when it rains,
that the same blood ran through our veins.
That the root of our bond could be explored
like that math problem in third grade
we could never figure out, but found
the answer to by cheating.

They thought because we all had brown
skin—excuse me, tan, not brown—I was
cool enough to have around. Tanning-bed
skin that wasn't just a trend, it was
a marker, a true sign of fitting in.

To all the girls who ever judged me:
I'm Mexican, I'm white, I'm brown,
I'm pale, I'm yellow, I'm sick of being down.
I'm all the shades you ever painted me as.
If the world was painted
using a box of crayons,
we'd run out of all the
brown, brown, browns.

Black Tigers

Taylor Thomas
First Place for High School Prose, 2016

When I was seven, my friend and I invented a game. We called it "Tigers," an activity that mostly involved a lot of crawling around and fake growling. "Ah! A black tiger! I don't like black tigers!" my friend shouted during one particular session of such a game, as I backed him into the corner of our classroom, growling and swiping with imaginary claws. I don't remember getting angry or upset with him, but what I do remember is my teacher holding me tight for a long time afterwards, as if trying to protect me from something, and telling me that it would never happen again. I'm not sure how severely my friend was punished, if at all, but I don't think that we played "Tigers" again after that. We were quite young at the time, but already we had established that there was a difference between the two of us: My friend was a tiger. I was a *black* tiger.

I didn't see the significance of this event until much later, when I heard someone claiming to be color-blind. Not the kind that makes it hard to tell red from green, but the kind that supposedly stops one from seeing race. It's silly to pretend that true "color blindness" can ever truly be achieved. To ask someone to enter a room *without* noticing the differences of the people around them is completely unreasonable. Back in prehistoric times, when we were constantly threatened by the natural world around us, noticing differences in one's environment is what kept us alive. Today, we continue to notice differences—whether consciously or unconsciously—not necessarily for survival, but rather so that we can assess and safely navigate through different social situations. We all do it, so why all of the fuss when it comes to race?

The color-blind perspective attempts to simplify a very complicated topic, and often comes from people who don't *have* to think about color. Because skin color has never been an issue *for them*, they decide it's not a real issue for anyone. They can simply bury their heads in the sand like ostriches and hope that maybe if we stop talking about the problem, it will go away on its own. But this is not the case. My childhood friend saw the difference between my skin and his. But then he went a step further and declared that he didn't like "tigers" like me. So the problem isn't acknowledging differences; the problem is valuing or treating people differently because of those differences. Those who label themselves as color-blind are attempting not to see color, but in reality, it is what allows them to avoid seeing injustices.

I can't really blame these ostriches for burying their heads in the sand. Talking about race is difficult for all parties involved. But I have also seen the alternative— complete and utter silence on both ends—and it isn't much better. I have attended a predominately white school for most of my life. And although silence around racial issues is not uncommon in this kind of school setting, I will admit that I have been lucky. Many black kids (especially black girls) struggle socially when they attend predominately white private schools. Fortunately, I have been able to thrive socially at my school, aside from a few bumps on the road here and there.

There was a time during my sophomore year when racial tensions were particularly high, and a few of my black sisters and I decided that we needed a day for us. Dressed in black, hair picks in our afros, we entered school the next day, a single unit, together in solidarity. It wasn't long before we were called into a meeting with our dean and the faculty advisor of our Black Student Union (BSU) on the grounds that several white classmates had felt "threatened" by our wearing black. The blatant racial stereotyping that had brought us into this meeting was only a small part of the problem.

We tried to explain what had brought us to this point, why we were dressed in black, and "scaring" the other students: the racially charged arguments in the school hallways, the white students' determination to ignore our concerns about their behavior, the angry Tweets when the in-school conflicts continued online. But the dean and BSU faculty advisor (who is black) were not convinced that our protest had merit, even when we described in detail the kinds of things we faced as black students amongst mostly white peers: the students' use of racial slurs in casual conversation; the boys who decided that white girls would always be better than black girls; the insistence by both staff and students that our issues weren't valid.

Once we had finished our stories, I clearly remember the BSU advisor making the following assertion: If we had not called attention to ourselves, *none of this would have happened.* And although this statement angered me to no end, to some extent, she was right. If we hadn't formed a Black Student Union, this would not have happened. If we hadn't forced our classmates to give a damn about race, this would not had happened. If we hadn't dressed in black, none of this would have happened.

But we did dress in black that day, and we did talk about race, and we did start a black student union, and I'm glad that we did. Because if we hadn't done those things, ostriches could stay ostriches, and our school's problems concerning race would never even get close to being resolved. Where our advisor was oh-so-very-wrong, however, was in believing that without our actions, the racial tension in our school would simply disappear. Perhaps, in the eyes of someone who does not come face-to-face with the injustices a black student can face, this is the case. But the absence of action does not eliminate conflict. It only masks it.

I don't blame the administration (at least not anymore), because I know that their job is to keep the peace. But the kind of attitude that our BSU advisor had—that we should avoid calling attention to ourselves—is a dangerous one. This attitude brings the peace that the administration wants so badly, but this kind of peace, as Dr. Martin Luther King, Jr., would describe it, is a "negative peace." It is a peace that allows white students to keep their heads in the sand and to condemn those of us who dare threaten the security of their willful ignorance. It is a peace that allows those in charge to only do what is necessary to calm rough waters without targeting the source of the problem. It is a peace that silences the voices of those who want to educate their peers but are afraid of creating conflict. It is a peace that values white feelings over the importance of black voices.

The shocking truth is that I am—whether people like it or not—a black tiger. No amount of willful ignorance or head-burying sand can change that. When it comes to the fight for social justice, accepting this is only the first step, and it is the only easy one. After that, the hard part is acknowledging that because we *aren't* color-blind and because we *do* see race, sometimes people are going to be treated differently and unfairly because of how they look. Confronting this unfair treatment is at the heart of the fight for social justice. To deny that differences and injustices exist is bad; to blame these injustices on those who speak out against them is even worse. Color blindness seeks to keep the voices of the oppressed quiet, and increase the volume of those who are comfortable with the racial status quo.

Joining the Black Student Union at my school has been a liberating experience for me because I did not have to pretend to be color-blind, and neither did the other club members. For the first time, I was surrounded by peers who supported me and who told me that it is okay to talk about being black in school and in America. Of course, as our BSU advisor had already pointed out for us, when we have these conversations we *are* going to call attention to ourselves. We *are* going to make waves. But I would rather be at the center of attention, at the heart of the battle, than be a spectator to a negative peace.

An Unforgettable Journey

Jamar Thrasher
First Place for High School Prose, 2003

I remember a brown globe that was always near me. The globe that I had as a child took me to far-off lands such as Iceland, Russia, Zimbabwe, Guatemala, and so many more. There were moments when I would stare at the globe for hours and wonder what it would be like to live in a place other than America.

In middle school I was faced with the harsh reality that I did not know my origin. Everyone in my class basically knew where they came from—whether it was Poland, Ireland, or Israel, they all knew where they came from. I knew I came from someplace, and that place was called Africa. I was in the art room at the time, and I listened to a student speak of being Jewish and speaking Hebrew. I did not know what my language was, but I knew that I had one. I also knew that somewhere in the motherland that I had family, that my ebony skin didn't shine like the warriors of a thousand tribes for nothing.

Years after my art class, I was a sophomore at the Pittsburgh High School for the Creative and Performing Arts. I was in English class when the student body was dismissed for an assembly. In the brown seats that filled the auditorium, I marveled at what I heard. The man standing on stage said any one of us could take the opportunity to make a trip to a new land. It was my chance, my chance to see a link of myself other than in America.

I had chosen Ghana as a country that I wanted to explore. It seemed interesting, and its culture of gold mines, tribes, and slave castles seemed rich. I was granted the opportunity to go to Ghana that summer by the Experiment in International Living. I nestled right in with my group. My group and I had been traveling and touring the country for a few weeks when we were notified that we were going to a slave castle.

Ghana has two slave castles: the Elmina Castle and the Cape Coast Castle. Both castles were fortresses of terror. They were holding places for human cargo. The Elmina Slave Castle was the one on our agenda today. The Elmina Castle was one of the first slave trading areas in Africa. It was constructed in 1482 by the Portuguese, but was then captured by the Dutch in 1673. The castle served a major role of trading with Brazil and the Caribbean. Now it is a place where tourists can come and see the harsh realities of slavery up close.

We stood outside of the castle. From the outside it looked marvelous. The architectural work was distinctive. The cannons that lined the wall and the drawbridge at the entrance of the castle let me see something real. We were at the Elmina Slave Castle. The slave castle was in Cape Coast, which is a city in Ghana that is a large fishing area. We walked over the top of the drawbridge and were met by the tour guide.

I wondered what I might learn that day. I was thinking over and over that I was probably standing on a spot where my relatives stood. I reminisced about the history of slavery that I had been taught, but this was something that had more significance than a textbook. I was actually somewhere that mattered. I was face-to-face with the ghost of tragedy.

The guide led my group—teenage students and a few adult leaders—to the dreadful dungeon where they held the male slaves. I imagined it: people packed as tight as sardines in a tin. The cramped space was not fit for anyone. The musty air filtered in and out, and the paint-chipped walls seemed like a border separating the pain of the slaves from the others. The guide told stories of men fighting for food, air, and life. The room was about the size of a city playground, but hundreds of bodies, souls, and lives were packed into the room. I felt sick because I could see and hear the cries of affliction. In the upper part of the dungeon was a hole. The hole let in light and air that barely helped.

The dungeon and its tears ripped my soul. The tour guide led us to a place behind the dungeon. He took us to a door where slaves could not return from. It was called the door of no return. The door was the right size for a child, but it was what the captives had to pass through. The door was closed, and I could see the light encompass the outside brim. The guide opened the door, and I looked through its battered frame, the same frame the 30,000 slaves had passed through by the 18th century. As a young African American male, there is not a lot that history books teach me about my heritage besides the occasional Civil Rights Movement chapters and sections on great motivators like Martin Luther King and Rosa Parks. This was probably going to be the closest to my ancestors as I would get. I could not pinpoint the exact African country my ancestors came from or their names—I only know that it all intertwined and passed through me. I did not have any direct relatives outside of the United States, but I know they exist. I do not have a special language that I grew up speaking in my home, but it seemed that I had found something. The group, the trip, and Ghana helped me realize that I also have a history.

Outside, the waves of the ocean splashed together in harmony. The breeze helped calm my soul. I had experienced something that I had not experienced before and I felt free! I felt free because I had something to remember.

Skin

Lynell Tomlin
Second Place for High School Poetry, 2012 (Tie)

Alexis said,
"I'm light-skinned.
I'm pretty because I'm light-skinned.
You're dark-skinned.
You're ugly because you're dark-skinned."
How about we run away.
How about we not worry about our skin.
How about we just are us.
How about we do our work and worry about pretty later.
How about we pay attention to the pros and not the cons.
How about we are ourselves.

Ryan Tuchin
Runner-up for High School Poetry, 2008

I was thinking of the time we walked down

Second Avenue with the rusted buildings

surrounding us and you carrying a sign with big

black letters: "Don't like gay marriage? Don't get one."

Do you remember the shouts that rang

from the avenue down to the point

where all three rivers meet, turning into the Ohio,

which I've always thought ran into the Mississippi?

The shouts of "screw gays" and "ain't no queers coming here"

rang from the lips of men with shaven heads

that glistened with sweat as we walked in front

of Heinz Hall, parallel to the Allegheny River.

One had a red swastika tattooed on the back of his neck

and the spit that came out of his mouth as he yelled landed

on the pavement next to your feet, and you looked at me,

lowering your sign slightly. I reached for your hand.

Black Girls

Cecilia Westbrook
First Place for College Prose, 2009

I grew up in a neighborhood on the south side of Chicago known for its diversity and its university. It was a little bastion of liberalism bordering on socialism, a crucible of free thought where all creeds and colors mixed. A Baptist university where atheist professors teach Jewish students, as my mom used to joke. It was a place where the exchange of ideas so valued seemed also hard-won, surrounded as it was by neighborhoods we didn't want to venture into at night, and prey to occasional burglary and bank robbing.

My brothers and I attended the upscale private school there, along with the other children of the staff and professors. My classmates were from all different backgrounds, were all different colors. It was the kind of school founded on Principles, and conducted according to them; a place where everybody was equal and they made sure we knew it. Racial and cultural equality were unquestionable. Martin Luther King, Jr. Day was celebrated with a great gala each year: an assembly, a parade, and a play. But it was not a forward-looking celebration filled with the rhetoric of hope and change and the continued progression of our nation. To the children of the Lab School, it seemed like a backward holiday; a reminiscence and a disavowal of the strange, crazy people who used to live in America. One year, my friends and I got in trouble for hiding under the bleachers and gossiping instead of paying attention. We were much more interested in the boy, Spencer, that Diana had a crush on.

I had a lot of friends growing up. I had white friends, Hispanic friends, Jewish friends, Indian friends, and Asian friends. Of all the classmates I would see in the yard at recess, the ones I remember most were the black girls. I was so jealous of them. I loved the way they tied their kinky hair back with the hair ties with colorful beads on them. They knew how to dance and all the best jumprope games, which I was mostly too uncoordinated to participate in. They had a way of saying their "T"s which I could never quite imitate; when they talked it was with an intensity and a fearlessness. The words just rolled out of them with a rhythm and a grace.

The year I turned twelve, my mom changed jobs and could no longer afford to send me to the hoity-toity private school. We moved to the north side, and I was enrolled in the best public school in the neighborhood. It was a place that rested proudly on its test scores, that lauded itself in school newsletters and assemblies and parent-teacher conferences, congratulating us students on being among the best-performing public school students in Chicago. When I got to my classes, I discovered I had already learned most of the material years before. I settled into a steady stream of "A"s and consigned myself to long afternoons of finishing homework early and reading a book instead.

There were black girls there, too. More of them, in fact. But most of them were not in my classes anymore. Our school was stratified by "gifted" level, with students divided into classes by performance level. I was near the top, and I remember seeing fewer and fewer black girls in my class each year. I would see them in the hallways, talking in their rhythm, carefully adjusting their elaborate, beautiful hairdos. They weren't my friends. This was not a place with Principles. My friends there were white kids.

In junior high, we all slowly grew up together. We grew breasts and facial hair, our voices cracked. I got dumpy and unpopular and even better at school. I did the history fair and the science fair and I almost went to regional one year. As the black girls grew up, the rhythm of their speech began to change; it became faster, angrier, more grating. Infused with slang to a point where I, the girl reading *Moby Dick* for fun, could no longer understand them when they talked. Not that they talked to me anyway.

I remember seeing them lean up against the lockers in the hallway, laughing to each other. This was the only time I saw them—they were not in the history fair or the science fair. One of them, in the year above me, got pregnant and was expelled for stabbing somebody. When the bell rang, they would be leaning against the lockers in the hallway while I would be headed home, carrying *Moby Dick*.

And when I went to public high school, I experienced racism directly for the first time. I had a friend, David, who was Hispanic but jokingly called himself a white kid. He was a hard worker, smart, and popular, but when we were outside of classes he would say things like the n-word. I was at first appalled, but he shrugged it off. He said he hated black people because they were gangbangers and drug dealers. David came from a working-class family; his father was a mechanic who ran a successful business that he'd built from the ground up in a deplorable neighborhood. Their family had spent many years dealing with racial tension and gangs. David was one of the best students in our grade. And the thing is, David was right—many of the black people in our school were in gangs, dealt drugs, and brought guns to classes. But then, many Hispanic people did too. And David had words for them, which were just as intolerant.

The great melting pot was high school gym class. It was not a class I liked much or did well in. I was still dumpy and bookish, and my first semester I got a C. Our gym classes were segregated by sex alone, which meant there were many black girls in mine, as well as Hispanic girls and white girls. We were united by a desire to skip out of as many activities as possible, and since our gym teacher was male, some of us spent as much as a quarter of the class sitting out, feigning "woman problems." It was in those long periods sitting on the bench or sometimes sneaking up to the locker room to smoke cigarettes that they taught me some of their slang. I would ask them things like what "boojy" meant, or what it means when somebody asks you "what it is?" and they would laugh and call me a funny little white girl.

But our friendship waned during the second semester, which was health class. This was a setting I was familiar with: a classroom, a textbook, and facts to learn and recite. There was no skipping out to smoke. Like I did in all my classes, I raised my hand frequently, aced the exams, and generally knew all of the answers. When the teacher called on my classmates, they would shrug and look unconcerned. They didn't know or care about the cardiovascular system, or VO2 max. The one time the teacher was genuinely able to connect with them was when it came time for sex ed. This was one topic the other girls in my class had a lot more experience with than I did: I was the only girl still a virgin in the class, and at least one of them had been pregnant once before. Confronted with this information (which was readily admitted the first day of the unit), our young teacher scrapped his planned abstinence talk, and instead one afternoon he passed around an empty Kleenex box and we had an anonymous question-and-answer session. Allowed now to speak in their own language, the girls asked serious questions using slang terms like "boofoo." Our teacher answered them frankly, blushing occasionally, and all the girls in the room listened in rapt attention.

As I sat there, for once uncomfortable and with nothing to contribute to the class discussion, I realized something about this speech, this language that the black girls had. I had always found it interesting, but over time I had found it more and more of a barrier between them and me—less understandable, more intimidating. It was like a verbal confrontation; in a world of things that made sense to me, things that I understood and understood how to understand, this was something I did not understand and had no headway into. It had frightened me.

But for the first time I realized what it must have felt like to them, the black girls. How they must have spent so many years sitting in classes taught in an incomprehensible language, confronting them with what they did not know. Watching the white kids around you understand it and succeed and be consistently rewarded. And, when you are marginalized like that, how enticing—or perhaps simply *necessary*—it must be to create your own language, something that you have that the *white kids* can't understand. This was not just the language of the black girls; it was the language shared by the Hispanic kids, and the working-class white kids. It was the language of the undereducated, of the underrepresented.

Now I'm in my last year of college, here at one of the most elite universities in the country. There are a lot of black girls here. They are in my classes; they have been my students, and my tutors. They are bright, enthusiastic, friendly, and wonderful. They, like me, like the Hispanic kids, like the white kids, like the Asian kids, like the Indian kids, and like everybody else, have all worked hard to get here and we are all on the same playing field. They speak with a rhythm, with an intensity and a fearlessness that makes me jealous of them once again.

But by and large, the black girls here are not the ones I met in high school gym class. Neither are the Hispanic kids or the Asian kids or the Indian kids—or the white kids. Our school had a 60 percent graduation rate (which was pretty good for a public school), and most of the graduates did not go on to college. I myself was forced to change schools by my parents, as they saw me slipping down into academic mediocrity. When I went to a magnet school, I met the black girls I would go to college with. Many of them had grown up in schools with Principles; some of them had also transferred out of terrible public schools after working extremely hard. These girls knew the language that I didn't understand, but when they spoke to me or to their teachers, they spoke my language—Standard English. So did David, one of the few people I knew in public school who ended up in college.

This year, we elected our first black man for President. Across the nation, there is the rhetoric of hope and change. This is an election I am proud of, and excited about, yet, to me, it raises a different point entirely. Our President-elect comes from the same neighborhood on the south side of Chicago where I grew up. He even used to shop at the same grocery store as us—what my mom used to jokingly call the Communist grocery store, since the lines were always long and the shelves were mostly empty. He and his family are black, and his daughters currently attend the same upscale private school where I spent the first twelve years of my life. When they move to Washington, they'll be about the same age as I was when I moved to public school. They are bright kids, and they will have a great future, without a doubt. But I wonder how much they know about the language of the black girls. That language is spoken all over the country, all the time, by people of all different races and creeds, but it was not spoken in the Lab School.

I think if he were to see our world today, Dr. Martin Luther King, Jr. would have mixed feelings. Our nation now is one still deeply divided, and the division largely follows racial lines. But the line itself is not a racial one: it is a line of under-education, of marginalization, of poverty. Nowadays, anybody can be successful, can have any job they like, can be involved in politics and shape the national conversation, but only if they speak our language. To all the people who were never taught it—no matter what race they are—those doors are largely closed.

Contributors' Notes

AMMA ABABIO is a sophomore at Harvard studying psychopathology and brain disorders in children. She is the program coordinator for three sites of the Harvard Chapter of the Strong Women, Strong Girls program. She also works as a mentor for Boston Refugee Youth Enrichment and the Alberta V. Scott Mentorship Program.

CONNIE AMOROSO graduated in 2004 from Carnegie Mellon University. She is the production manager at Carnegie Mellon University Press and a librarian at Carnegie Library of Pittsburgh. She is the mother of two boys and still lives in the Pittsburgh community where she grew up.

KATHERYN (CASEY) ARTZ attended Peabody High School. She received an honorable mention for prose in 2003.

RACHEL BELLOMA was a student at Pittsburgh Creative and Performing Arts High School (CAPA) when she received an honorable mention for prose in 2004 and won second place for prose in 2005.

MAYA BEST, a freshman at the University of Pittsburgh, studies English and plans to complete the Asian Studies Certificate with a focus in Japanese. She plays the flute in a music ensemble and is involved in FORGE, helping refugees adjust to life in Pittsburgh.

ASHLEY BIRT obtained an MA in Theater Arts from the University of Pittsburgh and an MDiv from Union Theological Seminary, where she received the Malcolm Boyd Veritas Award for social justice work for the LGBTQ community. She is Director of Christian Education at Rutgers Presbyterian Church and a regular contributor to *Believe Out Loud*.

REBECCA BORTMAN earned a BFA in communication design and a minor in creative writing at Carnegie Mellon. She is a designer and singer in San Francisco, where she is half of the band, Love, Jerks, and host of the podcast "Advice from Mom."

BRITTANY BOYD graduated from Howard University with a BA in English Literature. She relocated to the Pittsburgh area and works for Communities in Schools, a nonprofit focused on quality education for all students. Brittany continues to be passionate about writing and has recently written a web series called "#LWB (Living While Black)."

DJIBRIL BRANCHE is a sixteen-year-old from Pittsburgh, Pennsylvania, who claims his life isn't interesting enough to fill up a 50-word biography.

IRINA BUCUR won third place for high school poetry in 2016.

CONNIE CHAN lives in the Boston area. She recently tried to quit her job in the pharmaceutical industry but was talked out of it like a breakup with an insufferable soul mate. She is stably employed and pays her bills on time, but aspires to work in a creative industry (while still paying her bills on time).

BRIANNA KLINE COSTA writes about her family, race, sexuality, and other important matters in her life. She loves to perform her poetry and lead summits on the arts in social justice movements at local middle schools. Her ambition in life is to publish her writing and to provide more representation for Latino writers.

SHANE CREEPINGBEAR attended Antioch College, where he received a BA in Communications and Linguistics. He works at Antioch as the Associate Director of Admission and Multicultural Enrollment Coordinator. He remains committed to diversity initiatives in higher education, the immortal science of Marxism-Leninism, and his four young daughters.

KRISTEN DEASEY is currently a senior at Oakland Catholic High School in Pittsburgh and will attend Temple University to major in Entrepreneurship. She ultimately wants to start her own mental health nonprofit with the purpose of spreading awareness, resources, and hope to those struggling with mental disorders.

TERENCE DEGNAN is a poet. His most recent book of poems, *Still Something Rattles*, was published by Sock Monkey Press in September 2016. Terence produces the storytelling and poetry series, HOW TO BUILD A FIRE and Poets Settlement. He lives in Brooklyn with his wife and daughter.

PHALLON DEPANTE was a student at the Winchester Thurston School when she was named runner-up for high school prose in 2008.

JONATHAN DEVRIES completed his master's degree in urban planning and works as a planner in Manhattan. Although he works towards correcting transportation shortcomings, Jonathan is still passionate about poetry. He continues to express confusing (and often contradictory) emotions and experiences in poetic form.

MELANIE DIAZ holds a BA in English and a BA in Global Studies from Carnegie Mellon University. Her experiences as a Mexican American woman in East Los Angeles have inspired Melanie to dedicate her personal and professional lives to assisting the Latinx community both within the United States and abroad.

KATHLEEN DILLON was named honorable mention for high school poetry in 2004.

ERIKA DRAIN is currently a senior at Washington & Jefferson College, double majoring in biochemistry and Spanish. She has participated in medical volunteer trips, language tutoring, and undergraduate drug development research. This fall, she will begin pursuing a career in clinical pharmacy at the University of North Carolina.

BRIANNA DUNLEAVY lives in Tucson, Arizona, with her eight-year-old daughter, Eva. She works in real estate, but is completing a degree at Penn State World Campus and hopes to move into front-end web design. She writes music and performs as a blues rock artist.

ELSA ECKENRODE is a senior at Pittsburgh CAPA majoring in Literary Arts. She is active in the LGBTQ+ community and interns at Carnegie Library of Pittsburgh, Main. In fall of 2017, Elsa will begin the pre-pharmacy program at University of Pittsburgh.

DR. CAROLYN ELLIOTT is the editor of WITCH magazine and teaches INFLUENCE: a life-altering course on mastering practical magic. She's also the author of the cult-favorite creativity book *Awaken Your Genius*.

ALAYNA FRANKENBERRY is a lifelong Pittsburgher. She graduated from Carnegie Mellon in 2008 and now serves as the Manager of Content Strategy for BlueSky ETO.

GRETCHEN GALLY graduated from the Pittsburgh CAPA in 2007 with a major in creative writing. She completed a double degree in English Literature and Geosciences at Monash University in Melbourne, Australia, where she currently resides.

HANNAH GEISLER won first place for high school poetry 2016.

SUHAIL GHARAIBEH-GONZALEZ is a student at Pittsburgh CAPA 6-12, where he majors in Literary Arts. He has received acclaim for his poetry, prose, and dramatic writing, including the Scholastic National Gold Key for Poetry. A play of his, *The Righteous*, was produced in CAPA's Ten Minute Play Festival.

GILLIAN GOLDBERG graduated from Carnegie Mellon University in 2009. Since graduating, she has learned how to grow vegetables, slaughter animals, and drive draft horses on various farms in Pennsylvania, New York, and New England. She now lives in Champion, Pennsylvania, where she is starting her own farm.

KEVIN GONZÁLEZ is the author of *Cultural Studies* and the co-editor of *The New Census: An Anthology of Contemporary American Poetry*. He teaches at Carnegie Mellon University.

EMILY GREEN (TOVAH LEAH GREEN KIESERMAN) received Masters of Fine Arts Degrees in poetry from the University of Wisconsin and fiction from the University of Mississippi. She teaches at Ryder University.

MYA GREEN-WADE is now thirty years old and the mother of three beautiful children. She has been working for Mercy Behavioral Health for eleven years and currently serves as a Lead Counselor assisting young adults on their road to mental health recovery and overall wellness.

NICHOLAS HALL works as a technology consultant in the news industry. Although he never stopped writing, his literary efforts since college have been directed towards translating corporate jargon into English and back, largely in overlong, slightly florid emails. He recently returned to Pittsburgh and took a job with the city.

ARICA L. HAYES won third place for high school poetry in 2004.

DESIREE HENRY won first place for high school poetry in 2002.

LAUREN HIRATA moved to New York City after graduation from Carnegie Mellon to pursue a technical writing career. In her free time, she is the webmaster and editor for Foster Dogs, Inc., a nonprofit organization dedicated to finding foster homes for adoptable dogs. She lives in Brooklyn with her deaf dog, Lily Bean.

THOMAS HOLMES graduated from Wheaton College (Massachusetts) in 2016 with a BA in English and Film and New Media. He currently resides in the Pittsburgh area where he works as a filmmaker and videographer.

DANA HORTON won first place for high school poetry in 2007.

NATE HUBEL is a graduate of the University of Pittsburgh and the Winchester Thurston School. He is currently a graduate student at Drexel University, where he studies pathology and is training to become a physician extender. He tutors and conducts biomedical research involving liver cancer signaling.

AMANDA HUMINSKI teaches philosophy courses at Brooklyn College and provides management-consulting services to nonprofit clients. She lives in Brooklyn with her wife and enjoys cooking, powerlifting, and exploring all five boroughs.

RACHEL JARDINI graduated from Pittsburgh CAPA in 2009 and studied anthropology and Spanish at Temple University, where she worked with Philadelphia's immigrant community and received a grant to conduct research in Yucatán, Mexico. She has returned to Pittsburgh and is preparing to study local labor history in graduate school.

LEO JOHNSON won second place for high school poetry in 2013.

TAYLOR JOHNSON won second place for high school poetry in 2012.

KATY JUNE-FRIESEN is a doctoral student at the University of Maryland where she studies how news media represent place identity, from U.S. regions to urban neighborhoods. After Carnegie Mellon University, she received an MA from the Missouri School of Journalism and worked as a journalist covering media, history, arts, and culture.

JUSTIN KER was a student at Carnegie Mellon when he won honorable mention for poetry in 2003.

SIERRA LAVENTURE-VOLTZ won first place for high school prose in 2004.

KEVIN LEE is a Korean American from central New Jersey. He studied electrical and computer engineering major at Carnegie Mellon and is working as a Software Engineer at Facebook.

TYLER LEWIS is the director of messaging and project management for The Leadership Conference on Civil and Human Rights, as well as at The Leadership Conference Education Fund. In this role, he helps develop the organizations' strategic communications and messaging goals. He also works as a speechwriter.

ANG LI received an honorable mention for high school prose in 2004.

JESSE LIEBERFELD will graduate in May from Pomona College with a BA in philosophy, politics, and economics (PPE) and a minor in mathematics. He remains engaged in the fight for human rights in Israel-Palestine and plans to pursue a career in law. In his spare time he hosts a radio show for his campus station, KSPC.

SHAI MALLORY currently lives in the Washington D.C. metro area, where she works as a content editor and writer for *Astute Magazine*. She also works as an Administrative Specialist for a nonprofit organization that provides employment for the disabled.

KAT MANDEVILLE was a student at Carnegie Mellon when she won third place for college poetry in 2005.

SALLY MAO is the author of *Mad Honey Symposium* (Alice James Books, 2014) and *Oculus* (Graywolf Press, 2019). Her work has been published in the *Best American Poetry* and *Pushcart Prize* anthologies, as well as *A Public Space, Poetry, Tin House*, and others. She is a 2016-2017 Cullman Center fellow at the New York Public Library.

ANYA MARTIN is writer/director and Founding Artistic Director of Hiawatha Project, a company that creates theatrical works through movement, mythology and collective creation. She teaches directing at Carnegie Mellon University School of Drama where she received her BFA. Martin earned her MFA in Theater from Sarah Lawrence College.

CLAIRE MATWAY was a student at Pittsburgh CAPA when she won first place for high school poetry in 2010 and again in 2012. She studied at the University of Pittsburgh.

IMAN MAZLOUM is a Muslim woman of Indian, Ugandan, and Lebanese descent married to an Iranian she met while at Carnegie Mellon. She holds a Bachelors of Humanities and Arts in International Relations and Drama. Currently, she is working on her Masters of Arts Management at Heinz College.

MICHAEL MINGO is currently pursuing an MFA in poetry at the Johns Hopkins Writing Seminars. His work has appeared or is forthcoming in *Harpur Palate, Barnstorm, Cherry Tree*, and *Cheat River Review*, among others.

DEBORAH MONTI is a Pittsburgh native, currently studying at Yale, where she is a member of an improvisational comedy group and creates content for Herald Audio, the radio journalism segment of *The Yale Herald*. She studies history, with a focus on human rights and legal studies, and is considering a career in law or politics.

LESLIE M. MULLINS was a student at Carnegie Mellon when she was named an honorable mention for poetry in 2001.

EMILY NAGIN received her BA in Creative Writing from Carnegie Mellon in 2011 and her MFA in Fiction from the University of Michigan in 2015. Her work has appeared in *New Ohio Review, Main Street Rag*, and *Uncommon Core Fiction Anthology*. She is an editor at *Print Oriented Bastards* and teaches fiction at Pittsburgh CAPA.

JÉRI L. OGDEN studied Communication and Culture at Howard University before earning a Master's of Education from American University. She spent fives years teaching in Washington, D.C., and one year teaching in Abu Dhabi. Jeri has settled in Houston where she currently teaches English Language Arts at an elementary fine arts magnet school.

SHANQUAE PARKER was named an honorable mention for high school poetry in 2012.

ALEXIS PAYNE is a junior at Yale University majoring in English and African-American Studies. Born and raised in Pittsburgh, she is a graduate of Pittsburgh CAPA. She is a 2016 Young Arts Winner and a semifinalist in the 2017 O'Neill National Playwrights Conference.

BEN PELHAN was a student at Carnegie Mellon University when he won third place for college poetry in 2006. He received an MFA in Creative Writing from Louisiana State University and currently lives in London, England.

Justin Platek was a student at Pittsburgh CAPA when he received an honorable mention for poetry in 2006 and third place for poetry in 2007.

Bani Randhawa is a junior at Northwestern University studying economics and political science. On campus, she is involved with Women in Business and Alpha Kappa Psi. After graduation, she plans on pursuing a career in finance in New York.

Bridget Re won second place for high school prose in the MLK Day Writing Awards in 2014, and then went on to attend the University of Maine. She is currently pursuing a degree in Wildlife Ecology with a concentration in Conservation Biology.

Duncan Richer received first place for high school poetry in 2006.

Rachel Rothenberg won first place for high school prose in 2010.

Frances Ruiz has published three novels. Her debut novel, *Fairy Senses: Book One, The Key to Embralia*, and her third novel, *Pale Ants*, each placed as finalists in the Next Generation Indie Book Awards. Frances resides in her hometown of Asheville, North Carolina, where she works as a software developer.

Adam Saad won first place for high school prose in 2008.

Ari Schuman was a student at the Winchester Thurston School when he was named runner-up for high school prose in 2010. He is currently studying medicine at the University of Michigan Medical School.

Themba Searles was a student at the Winchester Thurston School when he received an honorable mention for prose in 2010.

Indhu Sekar was a student at Carnegie Mellon when she won second place for poetry in 2001.

Ashley Smith won second place for high school poetry in 2004.

Sarah Smith is the author of *I Live in a Hut,* the winner of the 2011 Cleveland State University Poetry Center First Book Prize. She is a graduate of the Michener Center for Writers at UT Austin and the Iowa Writers' Workshop.

Casey Spindler is an actor and producer, known for *Boneshaker* (2016), *The Enemy Within* (2010) and *After You Left* (2010). He is half of the Brooklyn roots rock duo NICKCASEY.

Javier Spivey is a musical theater major at Carnegie Mellon. He is a graduate of LaGuardia High School's drama program and Alvin Ailey's Junior Division. His last two plays, *Straight White Man* and *dios te bendiga*, were produced by CMU's annual PLAYGROUND festival. In 2015, he was named a U.S. Presidential Scholar in the Arts.

Kristen Swanson was a student at Carnegie Mellon when she won first place college poetry in 2013.

TAYLOR THOMAS is a graduate of Winchester Thurston School where she co-led the Black Student Union and the Feminist Student Union. In 2016, Taylor was accepted to the ACLU's Summer Institute. Taylor's work has been published in *Kidsburgh* and *Bitch* magazine. She is currently a student at the College of Wooster.

JAMAR THRASHER honed his writing skills at the Pittsburgh CAPA. His essay describes his experiences traveling to Ghana, where he was introduced to West African culture and saw remnants of the slave trade firsthand. He currently lives in Pennsylvania with his daughter and is the founding partner of Kennedy Blue Communications.

LYNELL TOMLIN was a student at the Neighborhood Academy when she won second place for poetry in 2012.

RYAN TUCHIN graduated from Pittsburgh CAPA in 2008 and studied comparative religions at Temple University. He returned to Pittsburgh in the summer of 2014 and currently works as a store manager for Starbucks. He lives with his wife, Ashley, their four-year-old daughter, Peyton, and their three dogs.

CECILIA WESTBROOK is an MD/PhD student at the University of Wisconsin–Madison. She studies the development of depression using fMRI and behavioral tasks, with a focus on understanding how at-risk individuals process stressful events in the brain. Her other passions include cooking, baking, hiking, and cats.